A
243.45
L 15 c
c.2

The Catholic Church
in a
Changing America

The Catholic Church
in a
Changing America

by
Francis J. Lally

LITTLE, BROWN AND COMPANY

BOSTON — TORONTO

NIHIL OBSTAT:
>Most Reverend Thomas J. Riley
>Diocesan Censor

IMPRIMATUR:
>✠ Richard Cardinal Cushing
>Archbishop of Boston

July 14, 1962

Published simultaneously in Canada
by Little, Brown & Company (Canada) Limited

PRINTED IN THE UNITED STATES OF AMERICA

Foreword

N ATIONAL elections were held in the United States in 1960, but many things happened beyond the election of a President. John F. Kennedy presented himself to the American public as a candidate for the Presidency with all the religious commitments his Catholic faith implied and conscious of the fact that his religion had been a hazard of considerable proportions to an earlier candidate in 1928 and had contributed in some measure to that candidate's defeat. Conditions in America, however, had changed a good deal in the interval, and the American people elected Mr. Kennedy to the highest office in the land. The process of the election itself had an educational effect, and its results continue to spread their influence in many directions.

This book suggests that a significant change has occurred both in the attitude most Americans take toward the Catholic Church and in the role of the Church in the life of the total community.

Undoubtedly other changes will come in the years ahead, and they will be significant for the Church and the Republic, but it is unlikely that the future will hold any change which will be dramatized on the national scene in the manner of those that occurred in the presidential year of 1960. What only the future can tell is whether Americans — Catholics and their neighbors — can turn the changes of the election year to that kind of advantage which will benefit in a permanent fashion the religious harmony of these United States.

F. J. L.

A portion of the material appearing in these pages was first presented as the Fenwick Lectures, at Holy Cross College, Worcester, Massachusetts, in the spring of 1961.

Contents

Foreword   v

1. The Church in America: A Catholic View   3

2. The Church in America: An Outside View   24

3. The Forces of Change   39

4. The Catalyst   53

5. The Shattered View   69

6. The Church and the Image   84

7. The New Look   97

8. The Education Issue: A Case in Point   125

The Catholic Church
in a
Changing America

The Church in America:
A Catholic View

CATHOLICS are fond of reminding their neighbors that America was discovered by one of their coreligionists. Perhaps it was Christopher Columbus who, in 1492, first came upon this continent, or it might have been earlier Viking sailors, or even Irish monks, who centuries before came down from the northland and left their traces in what is now America. At any rate, whatever their names and whatever their time, they were all Catholics.

Not only did Catholics discover America, but in large measure they were responsible for its exploration. This is a chapter in the pre-colonial history of our nation which Catholics never tire of reviewing. The extraordinary story of the French Jesuits and their explorations in northern and northwestern areas in the United States is not told in all American history books. Catholic children in parochial schools, however, read with delight Parkman's famous phrase, "not a bay was turned nor a river entered but a Jesuit led the way." American Catholics can identify the names of Father Marquette and Father DeSmet, but these priests are in no sense outstanding popular heroes in the story of our land as it is generally known.

The exploits of the Spanish Franciscans, a chapter far more familiar, occurred for the most part in the southern and southwestern part of the continent, an area which long after these events was added to the United States. The monuments left by these sturdy pioneers of the West have of course made it impossible for the memory of their achievements to be banished from the American mind. The very names of the cities and towns along our Pacific coast, from the city of Our Lady of the Angels at Los Angeles to the city of St. Francis at San Francisco, read like a Spanish litany. Unfortunately, most Americans consider this great age of exploration a picturesque, almost freakish period in American history instead of recognizing it as one full of glorious exploits which later bore rich fruit in the development of our life as a republic. For most Americans there are simply Christopher Columbus, Plymouth Rock, and very soon after this, George Washington.

Although Catholics played a large part in the discovery and exploration of this continent, they had very little part in its colonization. There was only one of the thirteen original colonies that could be called Catholic, and that one remained Catholic only for a short while. Catholics, however, think it significant that it was in Maryland, a scant thirty years after the landing of the Pilgrims on Plymouth Rock, that religious freedom had its legal beginnings in America. Historians may explain in many ways the reasons toleration was not merely possible but necessary in Maryland, but Catholics are sensitive to the fact that it was the only colony in those early years in which Catholics could live at peace with their neighbors.

The Maryland story is interesting and often quite misunderstood. Religious freedom was not guaranteed by the charter which Charles I granted in 1632 to Cecilius Calvert, a Catholic. In fact, referring specifically to the building of places of worship within the colony, the charter directs that they are "to be dedicated and consecrated according to the Ecclesiastical Laws of our Kingdom of England." Cecilius Calvert, Lord Baltimore, himself issued realistic instructions in 1633 to those Catholics sailing with him for the New World warning them not to take any action that might offend the Protestant majority. He urged that the Catholic colonists "suffer no scandal nor offence to be given to any of the Protestants, whereby any just complaint may heereafter be made, by them, in Virginea or in England, and that for that end, they cause all Acts of Romane Catholique Religion to be done as privately as may be, and that they instruct all the Romane Catholiques to be silent upon all occasions of discourse concerning matters of Religion."

The presence of Catholics living in peace with their neighbors in Maryland did not please large numbers of people in the various other colonies, especially neighboring

Virginia. As Puritan fortunes rose in England, Puritan feeling increased in America, and in the spring of 1642 the Virginia Assembly passed an act banning the presence of "popish recusants" in that colony. In 1647 the Massachusetts Bay Colony, nervous over the presence of the French to the north, passed similar legislation forbidding the residence of any "Jesuit or ecclesiasticall pson ordayned by ye authoritie of the pope."

So it was for practical reasons, as well as through conviction, that Lord Baltimore sought to put into law the religious toleration already existing in Maryland. "An Act Concerning Religion" was passed in April 1649, granting religious freedom to all "professing to believe in Jesus Christ." It should be remembered that Protestants joined Catholics in passing this Act.

It is plain that the Maryland Act did not grant wide religious liberty, but limited it to Christians only; yet even this, for that era, was a significant step forward. The Act, however, was short-lived. In 1654 the government of Maryland was overthrown by Virginia Puritans, and Catholics were immediately disenfranchised. Full religious liberty in the American colonies came first in Rhode Island and the Providence Plantations (1663), and later in Pennsylvania (1682).

Until the time of the Revolution, in fact, nearly every American colony had strict laws outlawing "papists." In Massachusetts, Catholics were hanged with Quakers on Boston Common for having dared to re-enter the Bay Colony after having been banished to the plantations in Providence. It is probable that not many Catholics came to America in this period, since they knew in advance that they were unwelcome; some authorities, however, estimate the number to be as many as a quarter of a million. Of those who did come, most lost their faith and drifted into the general stream of American Protestantism, as a result of persecution, discrimination, and lack of Catholic religious services of any kind. By the time of the War of Independence the number of Catholics in all the colonies was certainly not more than forty thousand, and probably a good deal less, in a population of four million. Most of these were the descendants of the original English settlers in Maryland; there were also some Irish, and certain pockets of German Catholics in Pennsylvania. With the War of Independence, however, a new chapter began for Catholics in the United States.

The Declaration of Independence had among its signers a Catholic who identified himself with his home address as Charles Carroll of Carrollton. Charles Carroll may be described as the first American Catholic who was called upon to defend his patriotism publicly. In the pages of the *Maryland Gazette* he was attacked by "Antillon" in 1773. This was three years after the Boston Massacre and the same year as the Boston Tea Party, and Carroll was defending the cause of the patriot party against the royal governor. To the open attack on his religion Carroll replied:

"What my speculative notions on religion may be, this is

neither the place nor time to declare; my political principles ought only to be questioned on the present occasion; surely they are constitutional, and have met, I hope, with the approbation of my countrymen; if so Antillon's aspersions will give me no uneasiness. He asks, who is this Citizen? A man, Antillon, of an independent fortune, one deeply interested in the prosperity of his country: a friend to liberty, a settled enemy to lawless prerogative. . . ."

The Army of Independence had Catholics in lowly and prominent positions, and General Washington was moved to pay tribute to the Catholic soldiers in the Continental Army. He received, as all know, important aid from Catholic powers overseas. Indeed, it is fair to say that the fortunes of American independence were decided by the skill of men like Lafayette, Kosciusko, and Pulaski, so many of whom came from lands of ancient Catholic tradition and were themselves Catholics. The help of the Catholic King of France, not a disinterested intrusion, may have been determining. The action of Rochambeau and De Grasse at Yorktown merely climaxed French efforts in favor of the Revolution.

American Catholics also recall with pride a communication sent to some of their number by the first President of the United States shortly after he took office. Concerning the Catholic contribution to the independence of the new republic President Washington wrote: "I presume that your fellow citizens will not forget the patriotic part which you took in the accomplishment of their revolution and the establishment of their government; or the important assistance which they have received from the nation in which the Roman Catholic religion is professed." Nor do Catholics forget that our first President, while General of the Army, outlawed in Cambridge that "ridiculous and childish custom of burning the Effigy of the pope" while celebrating Guy Fawkes Day.

Although the years that followed brought Catholics guarantees of religious freedom as never before, there were still serious disabilities in certain states. Some were non-legal in character, but they were nonetheless effective. The adoption of the Constitution in 1787 — two Catholics, Thomas FitzSimons and Daniel Carroll, were among its signers — did not totally remove the religious problem for Catholics in all the states. Not even the Bill of Rights in 1791 did this. But remedial action was begun in a serious way and gradually the constitutions of the various states came into line. Established churches remained established for a long time, however, in some of the states, and public support of religion was continued. Massachusetts did not disestablish the Congregational Church until 1833, and then only as a result of a dispute for power between the Congregationalists and the new Unitarian movement.

The growth of the Catholic Church in America in the decades immediately preceding the middle of the nineteenth century was enormous. For some years Irish immigration to America had been increasing. During the 1840's

Ireland had undergone a serious famine and the only hope for its people was emigration. Consequently, during the next decade nearly a million Irish came to America in a massive flood, bringing with them almost nothing except what they could carry in their hands. Even those who at home were propertied and had some resources did not have time or opportunity to realize their worth in exportable funds. They left with their young families, crowded into unsanitary and dangerous sailing vessels, and set out across the Atlantic to find a future in America. For the most part, the Irish remained where they landed. This was almost a necessity, considering their economic situation. The result was that Irish communities grew up in the middle years of the nineteenth century in nearly all the major large cities on the East coast from Boston to Savannah.

In the hundred-year period ending in 1920, some thirty-five million Europeans emigrated to America. The first wave (1820-1860) came from the British Isles and central Europe. The second mass immigration, from the close of the Civil War to the end of the century, included also northern and eastern Europeans. The third wave was even more polyglot and included southern Europeans. Each year the number of immigrants increased, until some years it topped a million. Of the thirty-five million new Americans, it may be estimated that one-half or more were Catholic. Undoubtedly, this influx is the most significant single fact in the story of the Catholic Church in America.

It was inevitable that large-scale immigration of this

kind would create resentments. They built up on almost every level. There were *social* resentments at the intrusion of this new and aggressive element into American society. There was the problem of slums and the substandard dwellings in which the newcomers were forced to live. There was the matter of language and custom and adaptation. From the *economic* point of view, on the one side the immigrant provided cheap and ready labor to an expanding America; on the other side he was competing with the existing force. *Politically,* also, the immigrants were a problem since, as the saying went, "they landed on Monday and voted on Tuesday."

Among the many immigrant groups, the Irish were almost the only people who spoke English as their own language. Quickly and visibly they penetrated their new country and adapted themselves to its ways. Reactions to their presence were soon felt.

In fact, some decades before the mass Irish immigration, anti-Irish, anti-Catholic organizations of various kinds, usually social in origin, had been formed. In 1834 a Catholic convent was burned to the ground by anti-Catholic elements in Charlestown, Massachusetts, and ten years later there were day-long riots between Catholics and Protestants in Philadelphia. As late as 1854, Father John Bapst was tarred and feathered and ridden on a rail out of Ellsworth, Maine, for his persistent missionary efforts.

An incident in Philadelphia in 1842 indicates the volatile nature of the religious climate in these years. Archbishop

Kenrick had petitioned the local public school board in favor of excluding Catholic children from forced reading of the King James translation of the Bible and participation in Protestant sectarian services. This modest complaint precipitated the founding of the American Protestant Association (A.P.A.) within a fortnight. "This association," says historian John Tracy Ellis, "was responsible for arousing antagonism between Protestants and Catholics and its agents were in good measure to blame for the public riots in May and July, 1844, in which thirteen citizens were killed, over fifty wounded, and two of Philadelphia's Catholic churches burned." Article II of the A.P.A. Constitution is illuminating:

"The objects of its formation, and for the attainment of which its efforts shall be directed, are —

"1. The union and encouragement of Protestant ministers of the gospel, to give to their several congregations instruction on the differences between Protestantism and Popery.

"2. To call attention to the necessity of a more extensive distribution, and thorough study of the Holy Scriptures.

"3. The circulation of books and tracts adapted to give information on the various errors of Popery in their history, tendency, and design.

"4. To awaken the attention of the community to the dangers which threaten the liberties, and the public and domestic institutions, of these United States from the assaults of Romanism."

The Know-Nothing party of the 1850's was merely a

transformation of these earlier anti-Catholic organizations into political terms. The excesses of this group, which was not insignificant nationally and locally sometimes a majority, soon led to its discrediting. The Massachusetts experience, in which the Know-Nothings controlled the legislature and instituted official convent visitations and other indignities, proved distasteful to the public, and their rejection was typical of a general disillusionment with this approach.

Americans became distracted after midcentury by the new and pressing issue of slavery and they further became involved in the desperate struggle of the War Between the States. One happy effect of the Civil War on the social scene was that so many Catholics had fought with distinction on both sides of the struggle that it was impossible for a long time seriously to challenge their patriotic sentiments. People in Maryland often mention the impact of the Daughters of Charity and other religious orders of women who at the close of battle cared for the sick, set up hospitals and dispensaries, and in many other ways earned their name of "angels of mercy." All this helped to lessen the social tensions which had been building up for decades between the Catholic Irish and their non-Catholic neighbors.

Although there had been a large German immigration, it caused a good deal less concern than that of the Irish. One of the reasons was that part of the German immigration was Protestant. But a more significant reason was that the

German immigrants did not settle in the East but largely penetrated into the Middle West, where they set up their own communities and were not so conspicuous among their neighbors as were their eastern Catholic counterparts. There may have been reasons of character as well, for it is noteworthy that on the day the churches of the Irish were attacked in Philadelphia, the German Catholic churches were unmolested.

Catholic troubles were far from over, however, since the latter half of the nineteenth century and the first decades of the twentieth century saw continued immigrations from other ancient Catholic lands. Catholics in large numbers came from eastern Europe — notably Poles and Lithuanians — and from southern Europe — especially Italians. Substantial Irish immigration continued until 1920, when the immigration quotas were finally set. The Know-Nothing party had disappeared and the Ku Klux Klan seemed to be gone, but the American Protective Association and similar groups effectually continued an earlier discrimination and brought it even into the present, since people now living can remember their activities.

That there was a "nativist" reaction to the arrival of the immigrants in that hundred-year period between 1820 and 1920 is not surprising. And it would be a mistake to suppose that all the problems were those of the people arriving; tremendous adjustments were required on the part of the people who were watching their own way of life being changed by the immigrant. Only the vastness of the country, its immense wealth and wide opportunity, saved the adjustment from being more difficult.

When the mass immigration was ended, there were in the United States a great many so-called hyphenated Americans: Irish-Americans, Italo-Americans, German-Americans, Polish-Americans, and so on. If the Church had been primarily concerned with keeping these people within the Catholic Church — and it is a tribute to the sturdy pioneer priests, for the most part themselves immigrants, that so few Catholics slipped from their traditional religious moorings — it had also, in the process of becoming itself one of America's great social institutions, been explaining and interpreting the traditions of the new land to those who were steeped in the lore of another land now left behind them.

Like the Civil War before them, World War I and World War II had a profound effect in uniting those of different religious, cultural, and geographical backgrounds. Whatever reservations we may have on the use of the term "melting pot" — and some reservations certainly should be had — a process of "Americanization" was going on. Every identifiable group in America was in some manner putting aside ancient and honored ways in order to assume those new qualities and characteristics which seemed to be the appropriate ones for this new land and this new time. As long as mass immigration continued, the process was bound to be slow, but once this immigration had ended, the trend became more obvious. The forces of social mobility, cultural interpenetration, prosperity, and education all had their effect in mingling Americans in new and significant ways, and divisions once considered important became less and less compelling. American Catholics, born in this country, did not consider themselves Irish Catholics or Italian Catholics or French Catholics. They were simply Catholic Americans.

In 1928 when the Catholic governor of New York, a man of exceptional gifts, ran for the Presidency, many people believed that the Americanization process had gone so far that his religion would not be a significant factor in determining his eligibility for that office. Whatever else may be said of that election, and the issues still remain quite unclear, we know that the presentation of a Catholic candidate at that time was, from the social point of view, decidedly premature. The campaign let loose on America a wave of anti-Catholic feeling which resurrected some of the ancient nastiness of the A.P.A. movement and the deep bitterness of the Know-Nothing party a century earlier.

World War II, by contrast, made an exceptionally effective contribution to better human relations. The experience of a personal confrontation within the armed forces between the Catholic and the Protestant, between the Northerner and the Southerner, between the urban and the rural, and even in some measure between the black and the white, unquestionably reduced long-standing prejudices.

By 1960 the Catholic Church in the United States had become the largest single denomination in America by a wide margin. It had grown from forty thousand Catholics at the time of the Declaration of Independence to a Church that could claim more than forty million followers. At the same time, American Catholics had built up the largest private school system in the whole world, on every level from the elementary school to the university. This in itself is an extraordinary story, and many historical forces influenced it. It may be seriously doubted that anything like the present Catholic educational system would exist if the traditional public schools of America had not shown themselves from the beginning to be unfriendly to the immigrant and dangerous to his religious upbringing. We do not often enough recall that the public school of the nineteenth century — and indeed in some small measure even in our own day — was a Protestant parochial school run under public auspices and that Catholic children were exposed to Protestant teachings and very often to Protestant religious services as well. Both in protest and for protection, Catholics built their own schools, at the same time doing what they could to remove the Protestant influence from the public school itself. For this reason Catholics must take their share of blame for the secularization of the American public school. When they sought to remove sectarian influence, they unintentionally assisted in removing religion altogether.

In this connection Archbishop John Ireland's suggestion, made some seventy years ago, deserves to be reviewed. Instead of erecting a costly and separate parochial school system the liberal and farseeing archbishop proposed a system in which the religious school would be part of the public school system. He himself inaugurated the arrangement in Faribault and Stillwater, Minnesota, although it had already been in use in some parts of New York, Georgia, New Jersey, Connecticut, and Pennsylvania. It was not unlike many proposals heard during the most recent debates on federal aid to education and certainly would have produced very different effects from those of the present divided system.

The local parochial schools were rented to the towns for $1.00 a year and much of their control was placed in public hands. Religious instruction was guaranteed, but it was held either before or after regular school hours. The schools took on some religious flavor — in fact, they were often staffed by teaching sisters — but they were nonetheless public schools, at least during those hours when the instruction was of a nonreligious nature.

Archbishop Ireland's position was roundly denounced by most public school educators, and some of his fellow Catholics were so distressed as to report the matter to Rome for judgment. Cardinal Gibbons, here as so often, came to the defense of the enthusiastic and original archbishop of St. Paul. The plan, however, never made significant progress.

We must not suppose that the immigrant who came to America was satisfied with the status that was his upon arrival. From the earliest years, promising young men and women made their way into the forefront of the business and political life of America. Great fortunes were made even in those early days, and Catholics were able to assume positions of high prominence in the state and national community. Two chief justices of the United States Supreme Court were Catholics and served over a long period with no murmur of complaint raised against them on religious grounds. In the realm of culture and the arts and in the learned professions, the Catholic contribution, every hazard considered, has been impressive even if not as large as many might have hoped. The major portion of the effort of the early years was necessarily directed toward the building of churches for religious services, seminaries for training the clergy, and schools for preserving the faith. If this may have seemed at times to be a never-ending, all-absorbing task, its very necessity gave it the quality of nobility.

While the Church had its difficulties from circumstances and people outside of itself, it was not without anxieties brought on by its own members.

The division among Catholic immigrants due to different national origins was a thorny problem from the earliest times. Each national tradition felt it necessary to claim a hegemony in Church leadership or at least demand some kind of "proportional representation" in the councils of the Church. Because the Irish outnumbered other groups, it was relatively easy for their clergy to assume positions in the American hierarchy, and bishops of Irish origin predominated in Church government. The resentment of other national groups in certain areas came to a climax in the years after 1885 in what came to be called "Cahenslyism."

Peter Paul Cahensly was a member of the Prussian parliament and an official of the St. Raphael Society, which was concerned with the care of German immigrants. After more than thirty priests had petitioned the Holy See in 1883, Cahensly entered for the Society in 1891 a plea that dioceses as well as parishes be set up along national lines. Thus there would be dioceses of German churches for Germans, French churches for the French, Polish churches for the Poles, and so on, each with a bishop of the congregations' national origin. The plea was supported with exaggerated claims of "leakage" of "ten million souls" from the Church, and the argument was that many Catholics were not being ministered to in the only language they could understand. The Lucerne Memorial, as the document was called, explained the expected good results of its plan to the Holy See in the sentence: "The poor emigrants will find on American soil their priests, their parishes, their schools, their societies, their language and thus cannot fail to extend the boundaries of the Kingdom of Jesus Christ on earth."

Certain Canadian Catholics also signed the Memorial and they were joined by the Prime Minister of Quebec. A vigorous protest by the American hierarchy followed at once and the Roman authorities dismissed the matter. It remained, however, for a long time a difficult and sensitive subject, and over the years certain minor defections occurred in the American Church along national, linguistic, racial, and cultural lines.

A matter which has been called the "most serious crisis in the whole history of American Catholicism" was an attempt to change the traditional Church government in favor of one plainly modeled on that of American Protestantism. It was called "trusteeism" and began very early in the history of the Church in this country. In some measure it can be explained by the lack of established authority in the earliest years and the immense territories which the first bishops were required to administer, often with very few clergymen to help.

As far back as 1786, "trusteeism" troubled John Carroll, who at that time held only limited ecclesiastical faculties. Members of a parish were often divided in their allegiance to certain clergymen and one group would seek to oust the favorite of its opponents. St. Peter's parish in New York City was such a place in 1786, and before peace could be restored by the arrival of a third priest, acceptable to all, a short period of schism had to be endured. A similar case involving German Catholics occurred in the first national parish ever established in the United States, Holy Trinity in Philadelphia in 1796. The lay trustees presumed to select their own pastor rather than accept the one sent them by their superior, Bishop John Carroll. Unhappily, in those days there were numerous vagrant and selfish priests seeking their "fortune" in the new land and they often encouraged the local laity against the lawful Church authorities. Holy Trinity parish, after appeals to civil law and other measures, at last went into schism and remained in that state for a half-dozen years.

In 1819 the trustees of the Catholic Church in Norfolk, Virginia, very nearly set up an independent church in protest against the "French" bishop of Baltimore. They appealed over the head of the bishop to Pope Pius VII, to the Congregation of Propaganda, to the state officials of Virginia, and finally to President Jefferson and the U.S. Congress. A long and kindly pastoral letter from Archbishop Marechal and the cooperation of Bishop England and others successfully steered the Church over these dangerous shoals. Later, when the Irish had priests and bishops of their own nationality, the danger from this source waned. The "trustee" question was definitively settled in the First Provincial Council of Baltimore in 1829.

At the present time the Catholic Church in America still reflects the various forces that went into its development. It still has, for example, some qualities of a minority Church, exhibited in the aggressive and uncertain attitudes which characterize people in this same situation. It is still a Church largely dominated by the Irish tradition and so has retained certain characteristics which are best understood in the light of that tradition. Although it is uniquely American, its origins are still visible in its life and action.

One thing is certain: the Church has found in the United States of America a climate which encourages its growth and expansion and a society in which the ideals of the Church and the ideals of the State are never seriously in conflict. It may be too much to say, but it has been asserted by many authorities, that there is no place in the world where the Catholic Church is stronger than here in a land where less than two hundred years ago it was under edict. America has certainly undergone a change in these two centuries; and the Church too has made its own appropriate adaptations.

❧ 2 ❧

The Church in America:
An Outside View

WHATEVER we have said about the factual history of the Church in the United States and in the days before the Republic, we must acknowledge that in the middle of the twentieth century the normally accepted view of the Catholic Church among most Americans is a very different thing from the view we have presented. For in the hundred years between 1850 and 1950 there developed in America a caricature of the Catholic Church which selected from the historic reality certain disparaging features, all having some validity, and from them made the present midcentury public image. Let us consider some of the prominent factors in this public view of the Church.

First of all, the Catholic Church in America seems to most people to be a basically foreign institution. They do not assert that it is un-American or anti-American, but rather that it is plainly non-American. This widely accepted view is not difficult to understand. In 1852, every member of the Catholic hierarchy serving at the First Plenary Council of Baltimore was foreign-born, and until very recently the majority of Catholics in America also were foreign-born. Moreover, the Church in the United States, although present from the earliest years of our country's existence, was not an indigenous religion. It was not founded here as was, let us say, Congregationalism or Unitarianism, nor was it ever established here, like Episcopalianism or Presbyterianism. It existed for the most part in only one original colony, which became the state of Maryland, and among certain foreign-language-speaking groups in other parts of the country. This air of "foreigner" — almost of intruder — was an especially important influence on social attitudes because it challenged the national consciousness which arose in the nineteenth century. People in these years were striving to understand and even attempting to put into a formula what it meant to be an American. This was a necessary and important step in our self-conscious development as a nation. The arrival of "newer races," as they were called, made it much more difficult to define "Americanism," and it may validly be said that the mass immigrations postponed such a formulation for nearly a century.

By its nature, the Church of these immigrants could not be assimilated as just one more sect; it was both non-Reformation and pre-Reformation. Furthermore, the native population had often been hostile, and memories of this

hostility impeded cordial relations. In almost all parts of the
United States before the founding of the Republic, the
Church had been the victim of persecution or, at the very
least, discrimination. Anti-papist laws in colonial times, as
we have seen, were commonplace. Events in the seventeenth
century increased the early anti-Catholic feeling. After 1690
the conflict between England and the Catholic powers of
France and Spain on the Continent made every Catholic
in the colonies suspect, and this feeling was reflected in
much of the legislation of the time, with its new restrictions
on Catholic life. In New England the fear of the Catholic
French to the north provided the occasion for strong laws
and extra caution in connection with the Indians who were
being converted by French priests.

The Church was represented even among learned men
in terms of contempt. When Paul Dudley established the
Dudlian lectures on religion at Harvard in 1650, one of
his purposes was "the detecting and convicting and expos-
ing the idolatry of the Roman Church, their tyranny,
usurpations, damnable heresies, fatal errors, abominable
superstitions, and other crying wickednesses in their high
places; and finally, [to show] that the Church of Rome is
that mystical Babylon, that woman of sin, that apostate
Church spoken of in the New Testament."

Later years and the experience of the Revolution mel-
lowed somewhat the common American attitude toward
Catholics, but a residual suspicion of them existed. Most
Americans had not yet encountered these strange, different

people against whom they had been warned for so many generations; they would at the least bear watching.

The early decades of the nineteenth century — for many reasons, including Protestant revivalism and Catholic bickering in public — saw an increase in attacks on the Church. At the First Provincial Council of Baltimore in 1829 the Bishops felt obliged to protest and to warn their people of the actions of the Protestant press of the day:

"Not only do they assail us and our institutions in a style of vituperation and offense, misrepresent our tenets, vilify our practices, repeat the hundred-times-refuted calumnies of the days of angry and bitter contention in other lands, but they have even denounced you and us as enemies to the liberties of the republic, and have openly proclaimed the fancied necessity of obstructing our progress, and of using their best efforts to extirpate our religion."

The image of "foreigner" was strengthened for many because the Church seemed to exalt its foreign ties, to boast its spiritual loyalty to the See of Peter, set in the theocratic Papal States. The ordinary American mind saw no distinction between spiritual and political loyalty to the papacy. The post-Reformation religious divisions had solidified the separation of northern and southern Europe. The Catholic Church, as a Roman and Latin institution, was not only something foreign but something traditionally feared.

A second factor in the caricature is so strongly related to the first as to be almost the other side of the coin. Along with being foreign by origin, the Church after 1850 was plainly immigrant by fact. The massive wave of Irish immigration to the United States during the Irish famine in the 1840's brought the largest influx of Catholics yet experienced by the young Republic. They came here in poverty, driven out of their own country by want, and they came with almost no technical skills, being for the most part a rural and uneducated people. The Irish were followed by the middle European immigrations, the Germans and the Slavs, and later by the southern European migrations, especially the Italians, and then those from eastern Europe, the Poles and Lithuanians. These successive waves of Catholic peoples rapidly increased the size of the Catholic Church to large and perceptibly expanding proportions.

The Church not only was made up of immigrants; it also exhibited characteristics which at that time were associated with the immigrant groups. It was thought of — as indeed it was — as a Church of the poor, a Church of the uncultivated and uneducated, and one having a large proportion of problem people.

Although there was a vast shortage of labor in the rapidly growing United States, and a beckoning frontier, many immigrants remained almost at the port of arrival and created serious situations in several East coast cities. Pauperism was one problem. In 1837 there were more than 100,000 paupers in the country; more than half were immigrants, who cost the citizens in excess of $4,000,000 yearly. It was not solely Catholics who were poor, but the Catholics were the most prominent in the general image of the impoverished immigrant.

The Church in these years also appeared to be an openly aggressive Church, composed of people determined to make their unacceptable ways prevail against whatever odds. The Irish and Germans were especially easy targets for this charge. Their social habits were repulsive in many respects. Temperance groups were quick to note that "they bring their grog shops like the frogs of Egypt upon us." Moreover, the sacredness of the Sabbath was somewhat differently observed by the various immigrant groups than by the older inhabitants. The "difference" of the immigrant was almost immediately apparent, and what was different was likely to be rejected and even feared.

It is no disgrace to the new arrivals to point out that both poverty and crime took a toll among their members. Some European states made no secret of emptying their jails and poorhouses by granting release if the inhabitants would go on to America. Most of the newcomers sought new opportunities and were fleeing the poverty of a life at home without promise. Long, unsanitary voyages across the ocean were a bad start and many an immigrant went from the ship to the hospital to be cared for at public expense. A New York almshouse commissioner sadly exclaimed: "Many of them [the immigrants] had far better been cast into the deep sea, than linger in the pangs of hunger, sickness and pain, to draw their last agonizing breath in the streets of New York." At midcentury one out of every thirty-two foreigners was on public dole and more than half the criminal offenses were being committed by foreign-born.

There was also a political angle, since the new arrivals were often met at the dock by the "bosses" and quickly registered as voters. The Democratic party got more than the lion's share of the new votes, but the Whigs also vied for the immigrant's favors. In Boston between 1850 and 1855, while the native vote increased by about 15 per cent, the foreign-born vote expanded by almost 200 per cent. This was an obvious and uncomfortable situation which was bound to produce unhappy reactions. In contemporary terms, one thinks of the South and all the emotions and implications involved in the "Negro vote." The actors bear different names but the drama is the same.

One can hardly be surprised that the new Americans, during these years, continued to look over their shoulder toward the "old country." If the Irish were not refighting the Battle of the Boyne, they were taking up collections to assist O'Connell; the Germans meanwhile, especially after 1848, were extolling the ideals of their revolution in contrast to the traditional American values. To many native Americans, who remembered with emotion the warnings of the first President about "entangling alliances," it seemed that the "American way," as they knew it, was doomed if the immigrant invasion was not somehow checked.

Economic factors — always significant — added to the caricature at midcentury and after. A period of inflation coinciding with immigration made the new American a scapegoat for the changing values of money. The Irish and Germans often had altercations over work opportunities, and both competed with the Yankee in an open and occasionally violent market. It is not hard to understand why many native elements banded together to protect themselves against the intruders by organizing groups like the Order of United Americans. In these seedbeds a later nativism was taking form.

The Catholic immigrants were for the most part a socially isolated people living in their own settlements and responding to the demands of their own people rather than to those of the larger general community. With our understanding of the sociology of the community, we can appreciate the impressive social forces that brought together those of like interest, background, and situations. Every instinct in the newcomer made his "ghetto" a home; it simply answered his needs and he felt secure in it. Unfriendly attitudes without helped to form the ghetto boundaries and strengthen the ghetto barriers, and little islands of immigrants began to dot the geography of America. They soon grew large, but they remained islands, with their few bridges to the mainland carefully guarded from both ends.

If we keep in mind that massive immigrations continued until 1920, we can get an idea of what an enduring process the foreign penetration of America was. The image of the Catholic Church during all these decades remained the image of an immigrant Church. Those who resented or those who were merely anxious about the changing face of the Republic had in the Church an identifiable institution against which these dispositions could be directed. Its size and success only aggravated anxiety and generated fears that America not only had failed to escape the problems of Europe but had acquired them multiplied. It would have been strange indeed, in this context, if the native and the newcomer were not mutually sensitive and mutually distrustful.

Native Americans also saw the Church in action as a flourishing institution in the life of the country; they experienced its vitality in day-to-day contacts. This power factor in the caricature has received marked attention of late. As the American public, largely Protestant, looked at the Catholic Church, it appeared to be a thoroughly authoritarian structure, quite different from the religion of their own practice. Far away in Rome was a mysterious figure called the Pope, who held final and complete authority over the Church and its members. Moreover in the late nineteenth century the Pontiff had been declared "infallible," a matter which was often misunderstood and a discordant note in an era of scientific and technological advances.

Pius IX, whose election to the papacy had gladdened "liberal" hearts all over the world, had become a vastly more conservative person after the revolts in the Papal States. The Italian nationalist leaders had become heroes at the expense of the papacy, which seemed to thwart all efforts for Italian unity. After 1870 and the seizure of the Papal States, the "prisoner Pope" appeared to many to be the last of a long line of colorful historic figures who were quite anachronistic in a "modern" world.

Many native Americans believed that this distant, non-American overlord made final decisions for Catholics and that his issues and decrees regulated many areas of their lives. This "non-democratic" feature troubled those who thought such religious obedience the kind of loyalty free men could not properly give to any person or institution. Moreover, the Catholic Church by its nature was a dogmatic Church and had articles of faith to which its members must assent. For many nineteenth-century Americans this was equivalent to abdication of reason.

On the local level a parallel pattern seemed to be repeated. Every large city had its bishop or archbishop; every section of a city had its prestigious parish priest. In those days the parish priest was a good deal more than a spiritual advisor to his flock. He was likely to be the best educated person in the Catholic community and a natural leader, around whom a somewhat bewildered people gathered for advice and direction on social, economic, political, and even personal questions. The new peoples in a strange land looked to their parishes for much more than the Mass and the sacraments and direction in their spiritual affairs. The parishes were social centers in the days when such facilities were not made available by public authority, and congregations gathered about them with an ethnic and often linguistic enthusiasm which is hard to imagine at this later time, when new media of communication have opened a wider world.

Many parishes, shortly after their establishment, began to build schools where young Catholic children, drawn out of the general community, were educated by religious teachers under the guidance of their own Church leaders. To an outsider this must have seemed an attempt at "thought control," or at least an influence whereby the new generation of young Americans would be certain to reflect in mind and attitudes the dispositions of those who had come from distant lands.

As the years passed, every important social phenomenon seems to have contributed to deepening the prevailing image of the Church. Non-Catholics were likely to get their information about the Church almost entirely from casual meetings with Catholics in the community or from records in the daily press. The latter source was particularly influential in preserving the caricature. There have been few Catholic newspapers of any size, and the daily press has been — and still is — largely controlled by non-Catholic funds. These papers were occasionally unfriendly, especially in earlier days, but even when they were friendly, it was not uncommon to find an unconscious misrepresentation and distortion in the news. The nature of news is that it presents the dramatic, the different, the sensational, and the troubled. We cannot expect to find an authentic and balanced chronicle of Church activity in the pages of the press; much Church life is almost without news value, being routine and unvaried. When the Catholic Church does get into the news it is usually because it has taken a stand on some social or political question which runs counter to the mood of the moment. Ten sermons on the love of God will pass unrecorded, but one sermon condemning the excesses at the local tavern can make the front pages. Time and again, American bishops who have spent decades in their dioceses building up an immensely fruitful religious leadership have received a national press only when, in some passing address, they have made comments on Christian modesty or taken exception to participation in "bathing beauty" contests. The simple fact is that almost any institution is likely to come off badly when measured by its press notices. The Catholic Church is no exception. Since most non-Catholic Americans meet the Church only in this manner, they are likely to feel that the Church seems to be strongest when loudest.

The moral teachings of the Church more quickly make headlines than other aspects of Church life. The condemnation of a film by the Legion of Decency, the placing of a book on the Index, directives on "birth control" — these are familiar newspaper items read by many who see no other facet of Catholic religious activity. The moral pronouncements are apt to appear censorious and the Church's chief function to be denunciation. In many American minds, long exposed to publicity of this type, the Catholic — especially the Irish Catholic — is classed as the heir of the Puritan or as the modern Jansenist. Undeniably this element of censure is present in Catholic life; it is the central position it assumes in the public image of the Church which constitutes the distortion.

A well-organized religious institution, with a careful hierarchy of function and authority, the Church is frequently pictured as a lobby or pressure group in social and political questions. Because Catholics are numerous and because their religious leaders often speak for them on certain public questions, the view that it is a monolithic machine, wealthy and powerful, is readily accepted by non-Catholics. A decade ago Paul Blanshard's first book, *American Freedom and Catholic Power,* convinced many Americans that this was the essential and fearful nature of the Church, and that it was a religious institution only in label. Since subconsciously a great number of Americans already considered the Church a power institution in society, a little persuasion along with some misrepresentation revived and reinforced the belief that it is something more than a spiritual power and is prepared to use its force in many directions.

Altogether, then, we can see how the Catholic Church in the United States, simply by its growth and its responses to the challenges of the passing years, presented itself to the

American public in terms which were not likely to make it either attractive or acceptable. From thousands to millions of members, from poverty to prosperity, from persecution to power, the Church in the course of a century had grown fantastically large, but it is questionable that it had become in the eyes of most of its neighbors a truly American institution. One who studies the history of these decades will appreciate that the Church leadership faced one serious problem after another in connection with the primary task of keeping the faith of the immigrant and assisting him in establishing in an almost totally Protestant milieu the ancient Christian Church. The magnitude of these problems absorbed all their efforts and turned the Catholic community in on itself. Only a few very farseeing men — one thinks of Archbishop Ireland and Cardinal Gibbons — realized the necessity of placing the Church in an American context which would be understandable also to the other religious groups in America.

The immigrant mentality, and the minority complex which was grafted upon it, were not conducive to what we today call good public relations. These people were seeking survival, security, and hope for new generations. Moreover, Catholics of almost every ethnic group had suffered at some time at the hands of the "natives," and one of their earliest resolves was to get along by themselves and to leave those unfriendly to them by themselves. All these social factors encouraged the isolation of the Catholic and the misunderstanding of his neighbor. Small wonder that even in our day it is still possible in some measure to pass off, as a true image of the Catholic Church, a strange caricature drawn out of the past which, if it once had a bit of historic relevance, no longer has anything like reality behind it.

The Forces of Change

THE WORD change when used in connection with the Catholic Church is easily misunderstood. While the Church as a social institution must adapt itself to the changing ways of every generation, it is Catholic teaching that there is a sense in which the Church is unchanging; it is set both in time and eternity. A mere glance at its institutional life makes evident that the present dimensions and operation of the Church are quite different from what they were when the apostles and disciples gathered about the Lord in Palestine. Similarly, the Church of the twentieth century must seem to many a far cry from the Church of the Catacombs, or the medieval Church, or even the Church of the Renaissance.

It is not an adequate explanation of the difference to say that each generation leaves its mark upon the life of the Church and that the accretions of the centuries change the appearance of this immense and historic institution as it passes through time. This exterior change is not the only change which the Catholic Church experiences. Even the *teachings* of the Church develop. Theologians tell us that the dogma of the Catholic Church evolves as new and deeper insights under God's guidance are provided. Thus the science of theology, through the ages, has seen the development of many new insights and implications in Christian teaching, such as those embodied in the immense writings of the fathers of the Church and of theologians of the stature of St. Thomas, St. Bonaventure, and St. Ambrose, all of whom probed the depths of Christian truth. But revelation, the faith handed to the apostles, is unchanging and once committed to the living Church cannot be altered. It is what we mean when we refer to a core of Christian teaching, a deposit of faith, the solid rock center of Christian belief which Christ himself delivered and which lives in the Church in Scripture and Tradition.

In our discussions of Catholic life and contemporary times in this book, we are speaking of change not in the sense of doctrinal developments, but of those new emphases within the Church which resulted from certain historic factors, social, political, and economic, and which gave new direction to Catholic thought by offering new challenges to settled Catholic ways.

The nineteenth century and the first half of our own century, a time of great historic change, saw the Church cast off ancient ways which seemed to bind it to an earlier culture. The decades between the days when Pius VI found himself a prisoner of Napoleon and the days when Leo XIII issued the first of the great social encyclicals, *Rerum Novarum,* were a period of immense contrast in the life of the Church. The change was brought about by the challenge of new ideas, and demonstrated the perennial ability of the Church to bring out of itself new answers to new questions.

The reign of Pope Pius IX, the longest in papal history, was a paradoxical symbol of this immense change. When Pius IX assumed the papacy in 1845 he was hailed the world over as one bringing a contemporary view to an ancient office. Very soon after assuming the papal chair, he inaugurated a series of reforms in the political structure of the Papal States which caught the attention and enthusiasm of progressive forces all over the world. This new liberal wind, however, blew for only a short time in the hoary halls of the papal palaces. The year of disillusionment was 1848, when Pius IX saw his secretary shot down at his side and he himself with a few companions was forced to flee for his life to Gaeta. When he returned to the Eternal City it was not under the banner of liberals or insurgents, but behind troops of the "old powers," and the young and liberal Pontiff began to see what unbridled political power could mean and the hostile aims of those wielding it. Harsh political realities began to temper the new liberal ideology. Eventually the Papal States became part of the new nation of Italy, and Pope Pius IX became the first "prisoner of the Vatican." In the meantime, the first

Vatican Council had been summoned with an eye to strengthening the institutional structure of the Church and demonstrating to the world both Catholic unity and strength. The declaration of the dogma of papal infallibility, consoling as it was for many Catholics, confirmed the popular view that the papacy was an obscurantist institution appropriate only to the Middle Ages. The rapprochement with the times appeared to have failed and the Church had set itself against "progress."

As we look back at those days we can understand why Pope Pius IX deemed it incumbent on him, as the Vicar of Christ, to gather the Church about him and to assert anew, in the midst of world denials, the unchanging truth of Christian teaching. When one recalls the unsteady years, as the eighteenth century closed and the nineteenth century began, in which the Church itself seemed doomed, it is easy to be sympathetic with every effort by Church authorities to tighten the lines of authority and strengthen the allegiance of Catholics to their faith. Moreover, the ideological mood of the nineteenth century was one which ran counter to every aspect of traditional Christian teaching. The emerging claims of science were used in almost every conceivable situation as a stick with which to beat the ancient claims of religion. The new learning, which brought with it the Higher Critics, was prepared to put the ax to the historical claims of the Scriptures and in this way to strike at the root of Christian belief. The innumerable social forces remaking society preoccupied man with the things of this world, seemingly to the exclusion of a proper concern for eternal verities. The rise of technology, the expanse of the cities, a growing industrialism — all these and many other factors distressed and disconcerted Church authorities and the comfortable practicing Christian as well.

In simplest terms, the nineteenth century was an age when the Catholic Church appeared to be totally out of tune with the times. This incompatibility was not a recent phenomenon; it had been growing up since the strange balance of the Middle Ages had been broken. The alienation which began in the Renaissance had continued to a bitter conclusion in the Reformation. Meanwhile the rise of the nation-states with their new wealth and their new economies had established a fresh pattern of power on the Continent and in the New World. On the surface, the fortunes of the Church may have appeared little changed in the eighteenth century; nevertheless, profound changes were occurring. The loss of the Catholic empires and the new claims of omnicompetence for the state drained the strength of the "spiritual power," and the Enlightenment hastened the victory of the secular over the spiritual, the claims of the "natural" man over the man redeemed by Christ. Moreover, the Church in these years produced no Pontiff of character assertive enough to move against the mounting tide of the secular power, which culminated in the suppression of the Jesuits in 1773 and in the excesses of the French Revolution; and having in a sense been "married" to one generation, she found herself "widowed" in the next.

Against this background the Church entered the nineteenth century alienated from the popular culture of the time, out of touch and out of sympathy with the new discoveries and the advances in technology, but always preserving and conserving those elements in her past which must be carried into the future. She often appeared to observers to be an ancient anachronism struggling for survival in a world in which she had no place. Before the nineteenth century ended, however, the process of adaptation was already so far advanced that a new religious resurgence was visible on the horizon and the relevance of the Church to contemporary Christian life could not be denied. The reforms of Pope Pius X, both liturgical and canonical, following so rapidly upon the intellectual revival encouraged by Leo XIII, brought the Church into the twentieth century with a quickened step and new vigor in apostolic endeavor. The "Syllabus" of Pius IX and the condemnation of Modernism by Pius X, instead of being steps into the past, were chastening disciplines which deepened the roots of Catholic action and strengthened the force of every Church effort. The extraordinary impetus which the encyclicals of Pope Leo gave to the formulation of a social and political philosophy suited to the age foretold the methods the Church would use to meet the foremost challenge of the next hundred years. Equally important, immense wells of spirituality had been tapped in the period following the Council of Trent — Rome's answer to the Reformation — and its revitalizing effect was felt in widening circles of Christian activity and in deeper understanding of traditional asceticism.

The notably farsighted leadership of Pius XI after World War I and his willingness to try new ways to advance the Christian apostolate on a world scale set a pattern which his successor, Pope Pius XII, continued energetically through a pontificate of two decades.

The century and a half which lies between the death of Pius VI, the Emperor's prisoner in the mountains of southern France, and the election of Pope John XXIII in the autumn of 1958 covers an astounding change in both the Church and the papacy. Measuring in human terms, it is probably fair to say that the papacy one hundred fifty years ago was at its lowest point of international power since the days of Peter, while today the Catholic Church is at the highest point of world prestige in its entire history.

Turning aside from this wider picture of the Church, let us examine what historic forces were at work in our own country to assist in producing meaningful changes in the mood and manners of the Church in our time. Besides that natural tension which sociologists say is bound to exist between a universal religion and the secular world, identifiable forces were operating within the Church itself to change it from the institution it was in the days of mass immigration to the institution it is in our era of a more mature national population.

Perhaps the most significant factor was universal education. In previous generations the Church in the United States, except in a few communities, was a Church of the lower income classes. The opportunities of an expanding America and the social mobility which a loosely wrought society made possible produced in a very short time a middle-class America in which Catholics everywhere took their place. Here education was the chief instrument of change. With security and affluence, with position and influence, came dissatisfaction with those elements of Church life which had been geared to a different social situation. The Catholic lay person in America saw his role in the Church change as his status in the community was modified.

Earlier the layman had been satisfied with making his contribution toward the proliferation of new Church institutions as they became necessary in new areas. With his improved education it became obvious that the clergy-laity relationship would have to be modified, since the layman, with his new maturity, desired a deeper involvement in the life of the Church both as a spiritual and as a social institution. The education of its members was warmly encouraged by the Church and in many cases was provided in its own schools and colleges, and the new aspirations of the layman were welcomed.

The present-day role of the laity in the United States is no unique phenomenon in the life of the Church. Pope Pius XI had carefully laid the foundation for this reform which his successor continued to emphasize. Pope Pius XII at his first public consistory for new cardinals in 1946 spoke as follows:

"The faithful, and more precisely the laity, are stationed in the front ranks of the life of the Church, and through them the Church is the living principle of human society. Consequently, they especially must have an ever clearer consciousness, not only of belonging to the Church, but of being the Church, that is, of being the community of the faithful on earth under the guidance of their common leader, the Pope, and the bishops in communion with him. They are the Church, and therefore even from the beginning, the faithful, with the consent of their bishops, have united in associations directed to the most diverse types of human activity. And the Holy See has never ceased to approve and praise them."

Catholic immigrants in the United States almost invariably sided with conservative political elements. In their home countries, especially on the Continent, they had often been victims of a hostile "liberalism," and when they arrived here they saw no reason to align themselves with the forces that had so lately been their enemies. Although there were occasions on which Catholics showed themselves to be sympathetic to the agencies of social reform, these were sporadic and mostly short-lived. We can point to the Bishops' statement issued in 1919 as an example, and to the work of some men like Archbishop Ireland and Cardinal Gibbons, but for the most part American Catholics as a group, at least up until New Deal times, could not be considered socially progressive. The labor movement, in which they were heavily involved, is an obvious and notable exception to this statement.

The Depression and the Roosevelt years which followed were a providential opportunity for Catholics, now for the most part second or third generation descendants of immigrants, to make their voices heard in changing the nation's social situation. American Catholics began to realize that the social teachings of the Pontiffs, even as far back as the days of Leo XIII, had been pointing in the direction of the social legislation which was being proposed for a stricken America. It was not until these years that we can speak in realistic terms of a widespread Catholic social consciousness and with it a willingness not simply to adapt to the community life but also to work to transform it. This move toward the more liberal point of view was very significant, because it changed the mood of American Catholics and provided them with a new assurance in public affairs which until that time had been nearly nonexistent. An official biography of Cardinal Spellman outlines his close association with President Roosevelt and his active role in American policy decisions, especially in the years after the death of Cardinal Mundelein, the President's friend in Chicago. The New York archbishop in the late 1930's offered Mass in the White House for what was probably the first time in American history. This was a new kind, almost a new level, of association, provoked by both the depression and war but also indicating a change in the "official" American attitude toward the Church, and, equally important, in the Church's disposition toward the government.

Another force in American Catholic experience which was working for change was what has come to be called "religious pluralism." For the most part, Irish and German and Italian and Slavic Catholics had always lived in the "old country" in a relatively homogeneous religious environment. They knew few Protestants, and what they knew about Protestantism was acquired more by hearsay than by actual contact with its adherents. How different was the situation in America! Here even those Catholics who lived in closed neighborhoods, almost ghettos, met their non-Catholic neighbors at work and in all the various community efforts in which they were involved. Moreover, they were living in a country whose majority was not of their faith, and they became acquainted at first hand with certain aspects of Protestant religious life.

Unfortunately, as mentioned earlier, not all of these contacts were friendly and not all of the impressions constructive. But despite the prevalent bitterness and prejudice toward the Catholic newcomer, in personal contact on a personal level the Catholic in America was apt to find his Protestant neighbor essentially a man of good will and very often a genuine friend in need. In most American settlements, especially those outside the large cities, the Catholic immigrant was impressed by those clear traditional virtues of honesty, candor, good living, and hard work which characterized Protestant life in this country, and he learned to respect both his Protestant neighbor and the religion which he practiced.

All this was bound to affect Catholic attitudes — bound also to put into the background those relics of bitterness which had been carried from faraway lands to America. From it would come that spirit of civic tolerance which respects the conscientious rights of others to worship God according to their traditions and beliefs. Not that the Catholic felt that all religions were of equal value in the sight of God or, in the old phrase, that "one religion is as good as another." If this had been his feeling, there were ample opportunities for mass defections, but these almost never occurred. What developed instead was a mutual respect based upon understanding, and a concern for the peace and good order of a mixed society.

This new religious experience may have made the Catholic Church in the United States mildly aggressive, but it also provided a respect among Catholics for the religious conscience of those whose traditions were different. There is surely a sense, in every religiously mixed society, in which one religion "tests" another merely by being a kind of competition in the same field. While we may not encourage such a situation on theological grounds, we may allow that it discourages the complacency which history has recorded in so many religiously homogeneous societies.

Foreign observers often speak of the "activism" of the Catholic community in the United States; by this word they mean to describe the incessant proliferation of programs and projects which marks parish life and even the wider Catholic life of the nation. Although the demands of an expanding institution may be the primary explanation of this phenomenon, certainly one other important factor is unwillingness to seem to be doing less for religion than one's neighbor of another religious tradition. The desire not to be outdone in goodness, as it were, is a praiseworthy by-product of our American religious pluralism.

The individual devotion of Catholics to the person of the Holy Father is traditional in all lands, but American Catholics seem to have a particularly strong regard for the Pope. Perhaps it has been accentuated by the history of the Church in this country, since the early attacks on Catholics were virulently anti-papist. It may be only because acknowledgment of the claims of the papacy is such a distinguishing mark among the religions of our plural society that Catholics so firmly and so ostentatiously express themselves on this aspect of Catholic life. Again, it may be the strong Irish tradition in official American Catholic structure which has carried into the consciousness of our people this special quality so familiar to students of Irish history. Whatever the causes, the devotion to the papacy is both profound and practical and it has become more personal since the days of Pius XII, the only person elected Pontiff who had ever visited this country.

Every changing mood of the American scene will have some effect on the American character and consequently on those Americans who make up the Catholic Church in the United States. The rapidly changing world picture will also make its contribution. What we need to remember is that the Church, while always functioning in an historic context, is an institution set in two worlds, and to judge it intelligently at any moment we must be sure we see its contemporary historic reality as well as its unchanging divine claims. Even in his Church, God works through the generations of men to effect his will in our world. Unless we understand this, and reckon with it, we cannot see the Church in America in those dimensions which are at once realistic and intelligible.

$\iff$ 4 $\iff$

The Catalyst

IN 1928, for the first time in the history of the American
Republic a major political party presented a Catholic
candidate for the Presidency of the United States. More
than fifty years earlier, in 1872, a group of independent
Democrats withdrew their support from the regular Democratic presidential candidate, Horace Greeley, and nominated a New York Catholic lawyer, Charles O'Connor.
O'Connor refused the honor, but his name remained on
the ballot and he received about 30,000 votes. The only
Catholic mentioned seriously in connection with a Republican nomination was the Civil War hero General Philip H.
Sheridan, who was boomed in 1880 but declined to be
considered.

The name and image of Governor Alfred Emanuel
Smith of New York are familiar to many living Americans.
From very modest beginnings in Brooklyn, Smith made
his way through the Assembly at Albany to establish an
outstanding record in his tenure as Chief Executive of

the Empire State. A man with a keen social sense as well as high administrative ability, Governor Smith was pushed for the presidential nomination in 1924 and was nominated on the first ballot in 1928. After a campaign marked by widespread bitterness on the religious and liquor issues he was defeated by an electoral vote of 444 to 87. The popular vote, however, was not unimpressive: 21,940,000 to 15,430,000.

Many factors were involved in the defeat of Governor Smith, among them his stand on Prohibition, which undoubtedly persuaded many voters. For large numbers of Americans, notably Baptists and Methodists, this was a religious as well as a social question but quite unrelated to the religious commitments of the candidate. It is now generally acknowledged that religion was an important but not the deciding factor in the 1928 election. During the campaign, however, an assault of major proportions was made against the Catholic Church in a nation-wide propaganda effort which was crude and unreasoned, and even occasionally obscene.

Of special interest from the point of view of this book is the fact that Governor Smith, with all his abilities and high reputation in his home state, in the year when he was presented to America at large, fulfilled almost perfectly the traditional American caricature of the Catholic politician in the United States. He wore as a sort of personal symbol a brown derby, and a cigar was also a prominent part of the picture. Moreover, he boasted of coming from the "sidewalks of New York" and was associated in the public view with the traditional New York political machine. In addition, he had a most extraordinary New York accent which characterized certain urban, and very often new urban, people of America. His opposition to Prohibition also agreed with the public image of immigrants and Catholics. There was no room in the White House, the majority of Americans decided, for the Democratic candidate.

Thus, in 1960, there were many Catholics, as well as others, who believed that it would be better for the Church, and certainly better for the peaceful religious climate of America, if religion could be kept out of the campaign. Many political observers also expressed the view that the 1928 experience was too recent and to propose another Catholic candidate, even three decades after Governor Smith, was premature. Those working in the field of intergroup relations had long been aware that just below the surface of American life were remnants of bitter prejudice which could erupt in a moment of crisis. Some of these people felt certain that the presentation of a Catholic candidate by either party would reopen the religious issue with all the divisiveness and unhappiness of the earlier campaign.

At the same time, it was clear that America had changed in many respects since the days of Calvin Coolidge. The national experience of a depression, the mingling of peoples in the vast efforts of World War II, the increased social mobility of Americans — these and many other forces had been slowly but effectively educating Americans to new understanding. The shift of much of rural America to the cities also brought a more widespread sophistication. Important, too, was the work of intergroup organizations like the National Conference of Christians and Jews, which was itself the happy by-product of the earlier religious crisis. A new maturity was discernible in American life, and minority groups of all kinds profited by it.

The Democratic standard bearer in 1960 was also a Catholic, but one who presented a very different image from that of his predecessor in 1928. In fact, he was different from all the traditional images that contemporary America had of the Catholic in American society. Senator Kennedy was young, attractive, and by every standard a typically self-confident young American man with a future. He was plainly not the son of immigrants; his father was well known as a former ambassador to Great Britain, a banker, and a highly successful businessman. Having attended from his earliest days what are regarded as the better schools, the Senator had received what many consider an ideal American education. He had also a record of heroic patriotism, having served not merely with distinction but with valor in the United States Navy during World War II. It was widely known that the candidate was a wealthy man, and this fact was used by those eager to defeat him. He conducted his campaign from his own plane and was surrounded by a large number of well-trained and highly intelligent experts. His voice was not a voice from the "sidewalks of New York" or any other sidewalk. It was in fact a clipped Boston Yankee accent.

All this made a picture with almost no touches that most Americans would recognize as traditionally Catholic. If the candidate had not insisted again and again upon his loyalty to the faith of his fathers, he could easily have passed for a young American of almost any religious persuasion. It would be impossible to overestimate, especially in these days of television and the extraordinary use of films, the effect this "image" had, if only subconsciously, on the mind of the American people.

The candidate also, on some questions, seemed to be taking a position that was not normally thought of as *the* Catholic position. For example, he never ceased reminding his constituents and the American public generally that he believed firmly in and was unalterably committed to the American constitutional arrangement of the separation of Church and State. American Catholics had many times expressed their acceptance — and their enthusiastic acceptance — of the provisions of the First Amendment. Archbishop Carroll, the first American bishop, had done so back in the days of the ratification of the Constitution. Every American bishop from that time to the present day had done the same. Nevertheless, there lingered in the minds of many non-Catholic Americans the vague suspicion that Catholics were never totally committed to separation of Church and State; that Catholic teaching properly understood favored a union of Church and State, such as exists in Spain.

The "separation of the two powers" is a long-established Catholic teaching, but so also is cooperation between the secular and spiritual societies. The human person, who is at once citizen and believer, cannot himself be "separated," although there is a clear distinction between these two terms which also implies separate areas of autonomy. The American constitutional arrangement is unique, as is the American experience, but it is quite in accord with Catholic social principles. These are the facts, but large numbers of Americans had the impression that Senator Kennedy was taking a position not shared by the majority of his American Catholic neighbors, or even officially by Church authorities.

A second matter that appeared to unsettle the American public was the Senator's firm statement that it was constitutionally impossible to provide federal funds to assist Church-related schools. The clear dispositions of the Supreme Court, as the President would say later, made it impossible for federal monies of any kind to be given to Church schools because such grants provided some species of establishment which was forbidden by the Constitution. By taking this position the Catholic candidate had placed himself athwart what seemed to be the ambitions of the American Catholic hierarchy, who had again and again expressed concern over the discriminations which prevented federal funds from assisting the education of children attending parochial and private schools.

Most people at this time were not able to make the distinction between those federal aids which were constitutionally acceptable and those which according to the more widespread interpretation were forbidden by the Constitution. The Bishops and the candidate were not truly in opposition, and as time developed, it became plain that the difficulty was to find a formula that would remove the discrimination charged by the Bishops and at the same time stay within the limitations set by the United States Constitution.

There was also a third unsettling matter, which caused more of a flurry among Protestants than among Catholics. This was the candidate's flat statement that when elected President of the United States he would not under any conditions appoint an American ambassador to the Vatican. Most American Catholics are likely to express satisfaction with the presence of a Myron Taylor, who was the personal representative of President Roosevelt at the Holy See, and they are likely to believe also that an American in Rome in such a capacity could probably gain information and understanding important for the American government, especially in its relationship with Iron Curtain countries. At the same time it has never been a topic on which American Catholics have had strong views; there was certainly nothing like a promotion of an official position by the hierarchy or the Catholic press.

Protestant feeling on the matter is quite different. When President Truman attempted to appoint General Mark Clark, a Protestant, as Ambassador to the Holy See, the Congress was deluged with mail opposing the appointment. Senator Kennedy was aware of this widespread disfavor and gave it as his reason for not making such an appointment. If he should be President, he promised, the very fact that the issue was divisive and an appointment would not be acceptable to a large body of Americans ruled it out as feasible. In his mind its unhappy effects outweighed its advantages.

These various statements in which the candidate appeared to be taking independent positions made many Americans consider him a person who would not take too seriously any political or social demands the American hierarchy might make if he were President. In many different ways and on many different occasions the candidate declared his independence of Church direction on matters concerned with the office of the President. All his decisions would be made in the national interest "without regard for outside religious pressures or dictates." "I do not speak for my Church on public matters," he said in addressing the ministers of Houston, Texas, "and the Church does not speak for me." So vehement was the stand taken on this question that many commentators believed that Kennedy had almost removed the legitimate claims of religion as an influence on public as well as private acts.

During the campaign there was by all accounts more anti-Catholic propaganda in circulation than in 1928. Its presentation, however, was not the same. In 1928, the American public had been subjected to propaganda that truly was scurrilous. It was "Maria Monk" all over again, with revelations of ecclesiastical excesses drawn out in morbid and totally offensive detail. Caricature and even pornography were commonplace. In 1960, the appeal to anti-Catholic prejudice was placed on a much higher level. It might be flagrantly offensive or clearly misrepresent the Catholic position, but it was presented in terms of so-called *issues*. It would treat such matters as separation of Church and State, the Church in Spain, persecutions of Protestants in Colombia, the Catholic hierarchy and public funds, the parochial schools and their divisiveness, and the totalitarian nature of the Catholic Church. Compared with what appeared in 1928, it was a highly reasoned approach and it represented an appeal to people of better educational background and somewhat higher sophistication than those to whom much of the earlier propaganda was addressed.

Many people awaited the inevitable moment in the campaign when the Protestant assault would have special force and point. This moment really never came, but something like the anticipated climax occurred when the so-called Peale statement was released for publication. Dr. Norman Vincent Peale, long-time promoter of Positive Thinking and a religious leader of considerable prestige in some circles, presented to the press a document which had been prepared by others and which he had endorsed. The organization sponsoring the meeting was called the "National Conference of Citizens for Religious Freedom" and besides Dr. Peale it included Dr. Daniel H. Poling of the *Christian Herald* and Dr. L. M. Bell, who along with being editor of *Christianity Today* is father-in-law to evangelist Billy Graham. Although not a long statement, it said in effect what had been said many times before: that a Catholic because of his specific religious commitments to the universal Church and the teachings of Catholicism could not in fact be a loyal American President.

The statement issued by Dr. Peale asked if it was "reasonable to assume that a Roman Catholic President would be able to withstand altogether the efforts of the hierarchy of his church to gain funds and favors for its schools and institutions and otherwise breach the wall of separation between church and state." For the National Conference of Citizens for Religious Freedom the key question was "whether it is in the best interests of our society for any church organization to attempt to exercise control over its members in political and civic affairs."

The most interesting and significant thing about the Peale report is not what it said but the speed with which it was repudiated by Dr. Peale himself and high Protestant authorities. Before Catholics could answer in any formal fashion the charges made in the document, high-placed Protestant leaders, like theologian Reinhold Niebuhr and

John C. Bennett of the Union Theological Seminary, had denounced them as misrepresenting Catholic teaching and as misrepresenting the authentic Protestant position as well. They spoke of "the failure in this attack at the Roman Catholic Church to realize the freedom of the Catholic layman in civil affairs." In general they described statements like the Peale report (and those of Protestants and Other Americans United for the Separation of Church and State, POAU) as loosing "the flood gates of bigotry clothed in the respectability of apparently rational argument."

It is hard to overestimate the importance of this repudiation, which very nearly crushed the assault of one wing of American Protestantism on the religious commitments of the Catholic candidate.

Near the end of October, another significant action was taken by responsible Protestant leaders. It had apparently been suggested by some that Reformation Sunday, which was the last Sunday of October and close to election day, might prove to be a good time for an all-out attack on the suitability of a Catholic for the Presidency of the United States. The plan was put in motion by conservative Protestant churchmen, often abetted by wealthy hate groups and special interests. The Fair Campaign Practices Committee, which has as its chairman Charles Taft, supplied the *New York Times* and other papers with stories and information on this plan in advance, so that responsible Protestant leadership was able to come forward in time and repudiate the whole project. There were places where, as a reaction against this attempted assault, Reformation Sunday was called Tolerance Sunday and sermons were given on the proper relationship of religion and politics.

Catholics for their part also took an assortment of poses during the campaign which had effects in one direction or another. Among Catholic conservatives there was strong support for Vice President Nixon. These conservatives believed that Senator Kennedy's record in the Congress, and especially his friendliness with liberal elements in the Democratic party, made him a dangerous candidate and they were candid in their opposition to him. Moreover, the impressive record of Vice President Nixon on the subject of Communism also affected certain Catholics who had strong feelings on the Red threat both at home and abroad. Notable among these groups was Father Juniper Carol, a Franciscan from New Jersey, whose article in *Human Events* was widely circulated. The title of his paper was "Kennedy for President? A Roman Catholic Priest Says No!" The liberal record of the Democratic candidate predicted an administration of "liberal ideologies" and "a gradual surrender of our Constitutional sovereignties." There would also be a "crawling appeasement" of the Communists. Certain Catholic papers could be identified as anti-Kennedy. The *Tablet* of Brooklyn, popular right-wing Catholic diocesan weekly, was so charged in other portions of the Catholic press. There was also a group of "too soon" Catholics who felt that this was not the time for any Catholic candidate to be presented; this minority timidity was not widespread and not unexpected.

An exceptional and significant event among Catholics was the issuance, by one hundred sixty-two prominent Catholic laymen, of a statement on politics and religious liberty. Because it was said in some circles that the President was following a "liberal" line which was in effect at variance with traditional and proper Catholic teaching, these laymen, without consulting ecclesiastical authority, issued a statement which endorsed the President's views and asserted that they were the views prevailing among Catholic intellectuals in the United States. This may well have been the first time that a group of lay Catholics issued a statement of ideological position close to the domain of theology without consulting ecclesiastics for guidance. While it was not — and was not intended to be — a daring statement, its issuance was a new experience for Catholic lay leadership on a national level.

An incident that could have had serious effects on the election occurred in Puerto Rico. The Puerto Rican bishops, in connection with elections on the island, issued statements in which they advised their people not to vote for the party of Muñoz Marin because of his stand on sterilization, birth control, and the teaching of religion in the Puerto Rican schools. Although this whole incident was surrounded with confusion, it did seem to play into the hands of those who maintained that the Catholic hierarchy entered the political scene whenever they found a pretext and claimed the right to direct the votes of Catholic people. Persons who reflected on the situation realized that the matter was not so simple. No Church, Catholic or Protestant, had ever denied itself, or allowed others to deny, the right to stand in judgment on the world about it, whether the scene was political or social or economic. American religious leadership had often spoken on moral questions, and our national experiment with Prohibition was a classic example. At the same time the Puerto Rican directive could not be lightly set aside, and it was not until Archbishop Egidio Vagnozzi, the Apostolic Delegate to the United States, and Cardinal Cushing of Boston had been heard on the subject that both Catholics and their neighbors were able to breathe easier. The Cardinal said:

"Our American tradition has always encouraged the discussion of moral and religious questions in helping to form the intelligent decision of the voter. Our attitudes on various moral questions, whether it be gambling or liquor, or sterilization or euthanasia, or whatever else, are expected to influence our decisions in choosing candidates and parties and programs in the public life of our country. The religious disposition of our people, in the American way, has its say in helping the individual voter form his conscience and use his ballot in keeping with his conscience thus informed.

"With all of this said, however, we must repeat that, whatever may be the custom elsewhere, the American tradition, of which Catholics form so loyal a part, is satisfied simply to call to public attention moral questions with their implications and leave to the conscience of the people the specific political decision which comes in the act of voting."

At last the election came and the votes were counted. Political analysts from that day on have been trying to explain which groups in America did in fact vote for the Catholic candidate and why. A fortnight after the election, *Life* magazine spoke of "a three-quarters solid Catholic vote which registered hardest where it counted most in the electoral college, i.e. New England, New York, Pennsylvania and Illinois." The *New York Times* in a survey of the election results gave anti-Catholic feeling as the reason for Kennedy's losing Oklahoma, Tennessee, and Kentucky; it was a factor also, according to the *Times,* in Florida, Virginia, Wisconsin, and Ohio.

As time has passed, more precise judgments have been possible. Walter Lippmann, a friendly observer, claimed that the candidate's Catholic religion lost him 5,000,000 votes. A more conservative estimate, carefully documented in a statistical fashion, was published from studies made at the University of Michigan. The conclusion here was that Kennedy's religion lost him 1,500,000 votes.

Whatever the polls and analyses finally may show, it is true that a Catholic President was not elected simply, or even principally, by Catholics, but by large numbers of Protestants and others in the United States. These were moved by considerations other than those of religion, at least as the prevailing factor. There is no explanation for southern states of immense Protestant Fundamentalist majority giving their electoral votes to the Catholic candidate except the fact that for them, often despite the appeals of their own religious leadership, the religious issue was at least a secondary item. Moreover, it is plain that in large urban centers liberal Protestants in great numbers voted for President Kennedy, as did the Jewish traditionally Democratically inclined block. One can conclude safely that, with many factors at work, it was a healthy cross-section of Americans in 1960 who for the first time chose a member of a minority religious group as President of the United States.

The Shattered View

FROM the early months of 1960, Americans were forced to become interested in the relation between religion and politics. The responsible issue was whether a Catholic could be put in the White House, and the matter was resolved beyond dispute by the election of the Catholic candidate in November. In this sense the topic no longer needs to be discussed, although many of the factors at work in that election have not been thoroughly analyzed. At any rate, the question that vexed us in 1960 has been answered: we know that a candidate from a minority religious group can be elected President of the United States.

But what is the answer to the companion query: what effect did the election have on religion in the United States? This may be a more important question than the first, for the answer to it may indicate that we have turned a corner in our pluralistic religious relationships in the United States. If we have indeed done so, that accomplishment is more momentous than the election of a person belonging to a minority group to the highest office in the land.

A national political campaign is a matter of great social significance in the United States and it has marked effects on the American community. It is not possible to expose both men and issues to the protracted scrutiny required in national elections without leaving a profound impression on the public mind of America. We have not often been able to measure just what or how powerful the effects of a campaign have been, but the campaign which emphasized the relation between religion and politics offered special opportunity to do so.

In general the raising of the religious issue revealed two opposing attitudes among the voters. Some made up their minds shortly after the campaign began that religion was extraneous to the election and the religion of the candidate was his private concern only. At first, this seemed to many to be the proper and even traditional American view. Its proponents argued that religion helps a man to be a good man, and so a man with definite religious beliefs might well be a better candidate than a man with no religion; but whatever a candidate's religious commitments they should be of no concern to the American voter because they would not, and indeed should not in any circumstance, influence his political or, specifically, presidential decisions. This point of view had a natural attractiveness, and some people were at first taken with it — it seemed to answer the problems of the hour so well. If a man's religion was his own business and not a proper subject for public discussion, the matter could be dropped from the start.

Many thoughtful people, however, took a quite contradictory view. Unless a man's religion was so meaningful in his life as to affect his decisions on every level, he was not a truly religious man. It was a mistake and indeed a modern heresy, these people argued, to suppose that it was possible or right to restrict the Church to the sanctuary and to limit the religious influence of the Churches to that single day each week when men normally worshiped together. The religious tradition of the western world was very different. A man's religious life and the intensity of that life should be part of his whole being and it should give direction in some measure to all his conscious actions and decisions.

But if a man's religion was going to influence his public acts, in just what manner would this influence affect others? Would it be manifested merely in the "goodness" which we associate with organized religion? Or would the public official attempt to impose on the larger civil community certain religious views to which he as a private citizen was committed? This question soon made it necessary to distinguish between what were described as specifically sectarian elements and the wider claims of religion itself. This distinction sought to separate those common elements which seemed to be shared by most if not all religions and those particular beliefs which might be held by only one or more religious groups.

This second view was a harder theory to live with, and it raised serious problems. First among them was the specific question of the influence of a man's religion on his public acts as President of the United States. Although most people now saw this question in terms of a Catholic in the White House, it was a very old proposition and it applied to all men of confirmed religious persuasion. If a Catholic in the White House might have some problems in connection with birth control legislation or the Vatican, a Baptist might have parallel problems in connection with liquor and gambling, or a Quaker might conceivably be involved in the issues of war and peace. This was not a problem of a single person but the problem of every public servant who accepted a set of religious beliefs.

As time and the campaign went on, it became clear that most Americans, even those who had originally subscribed to the view that a candidate's religion is irrelevant, were now more often thinking in terms of the second theory. Religion *was* a proper subject for discussion and it began to be discussed, sporadically and unevenly. The totally reasonable voices may have been drowned out by the clamor of the more numerous excited and fearful, but there were on all sides men of stature and influence who kept the argument on a somewhat even keel. The American public did not panic or develop hysteria; they listened with great interest, perhaps not always understanding the more complex matters, but satisfying themselves to some degree on the principal issue. The election campaign in this way impressed itself on all by reviewing certain religious attitudes, testing them, and modifying them.

We shall speak first of the manner in which the campaign effects, as religious phenomena, touched the Protestant American majority. For the first time in the history of the Catholic Church in America, Catholic teaching on many special subjects was discussed freely and candidly in the leading newspapers and journals of America. Previously, space had rarely been given in such publications to serious discussion of specifically Catholic teachings on social, political, and moral questions. Catholics, of course, were rather well informed on these subjects. The Catholic press and the large Catholic literature over the years had presented with understandable frequency the relation of Church and State, the basic tenets of Catholic political theory, and so on. In 1960, however, for the first time, American Protestants were exposed to a wide-ranging, intelligible, and often sympathetic discussion of Catholic doctrine.

Many Catholics during these days had the experience of hearing their Protestant friends exclaim that this was the first time they had understood the fundamentals of the Catholic position on religious education, birth control, federal aid, and other issues. An immense task of public education was being accomplished in such a way as to bring a wider understanding of the Catholic Church to the American public at large. The characteristic fairness of Americans saw to it that in unfriendly areas where Catholics and the Catholic position seemed to be under attack, equal time and equal space were provided for Catholic rejoinders and for explanations of the true position of the Church on vexing questions. No one can estimate the direct fruits of this exposure in terms of votes, but one thing is sure: many ancient illusions were dispelled simply by the dissemination of authentic information on religious matters into areas formerly closed against it.

A second effect, and a staggering one to some Protestants in the United States, was the realization that within the Church there was a vast area of disagreement, that on many social and political questions Catholics were quite as much divided as were their Protestant neighbors. This was a highly important revelation since unfriendly propaganda over many years had built up the concept that the Catholic Church is a monolithic organization. Because of its authoritarian structure it was thought to have, at least on all questions of consequence, only one point of view, with no difference of opinion permitted. Now it became plain that Catholics were divided on many political and social questions between those who could be described as conservative and those who were easily classified as liberal. Some Catholics, as we have mentioned, were quick to point out that they considered the candidate who was a

Catholic much too liberal for their confidence, and for this as well as other reasons there were a not inconsiderable number of "Catholics for Nixon."

Moreover, in the discussion of Catholic teaching and its application to the present American realities, it was clear that not all members of the Church applied the "eternal" principles to the changing facts in precisely the same manner. There was a whole spectrum of opinion, with some who had not yet quite accepted the social encyclicals at one extreme and what appeared to many to be Catholic "socialists" at the other. There was a wide space between the *National Review* and *Commonweal,* both edited by Catholics. Again one cannot estimate just what effect this new understanding of the Catholic situation may have had on the general Protestant population. One can suppose that it at least assisted in removing one more misunderstanding between Catholics and their neighbors.

A third effect on Protestant thought and action was related to the election result, which ended the long-standing, historic claim of Protestantism on the Presidency itself. No President of the United States had been anything but Protestant, and sociologists had often referred to the Presidency as a "status symbol" for American Protestantism. In their terminology it was a WASP token: White Anglo-Saxon Protestant. As long as the Presidency of the United States was limited to the people who could qualify under this title, America was and would remain, in name at least, a Protestant country. With the election of an Irish-

American Catholic the symbol was effectively and permanently demolished. Undoubtedly, this whole matter was more a subconscious element in the thinking of American Protestants than one to which they gave conscious attention, and it is possible to overemphasize it. At the same time, the outcome of the election carried many historic satisfactions, and the election of a Catholic President did have the effect of making America, from the world's point of view, a religiously neutral country.

Another effect of the campaign on Protestants in America came from the exposure of the friendliness toward Catholics that existed among many Protestants highly situated within their own churches. It was a surprise to many people to learn, for example, that Protestant theologians of highest quality had a long-standing friendly relationship with some of their opposite numbers in the Catholic Church, and that high-level Protestant leadership was very well disposed toward Catholics in many American communities. Numerous elements in Protestant life had long ago disassociated themselves from what was thought to be the necessary traditional antagonism against the Catholic Church. During the last decades, there had been building up almost without public knowledge a friendly relationship between well-informed and sympathetic Catholics and Protestants which could not be dispelled by the excitement of the election but which could, and did, make a contribution to public understanding in this time of crisis.

In this connection one must mention the efforts of the

Fund for the Republic, which at an historic session in May 1958 brought together in a religious seminar most of the competing factions of American religious life. From this beginning an effective "dialogue" was set in motion whose force is still being felt.

What were the effects of the election on the Catholic Church in America and on Catholics generally? First of all, every Catholic must have stood a bit straighter the morning after the election of Senator Kennedy as President of the United States. If only subconsciously, each Catholic was aware that at that moment a stigma of second-class citizenship had been removed. With the sensitivity to be expected in a minority religious group, Catholics had always been unhappy about the fact that their coreligionists might be called to labor and serve in almost every other level of American life, but one area, the highest, appeared closed to them. There was an inner resentment against this situation, and even those Catholics who conscientiously had voted for Vice President Nixon must have felt a sense of social relief when the Catholic candidate was in fact elected. A minority came into its own, and this could not be ignored by its forty million people. Other minority groups may perhaps have shared some vicarious "release" at the same moment.

This first effect had from the beginning a desirable by-product. Because Catholics now had acquired political equality with all their neighbors, they experienced a quickened sense of civic responsibility. When they had the feeling that they were being excluded from the making of the major decisions in American public life, they might have been forgiven for showing little personal concern about them. Now that these matters in a new way were truly their responsibility, Catholics felt called to a more eager participation, along with all other Americans, in the decisive political life of America.

It is too early to document this new attitude in any persuasive fashion, but as a psychological mood it came directly out of the new feeling of having politically arrived. It coincided, to be sure, with a moment when educated and responsible Catholics were on hand to accept the opportunity and take advantage of it. This should not be interpreted to mean that Catholics expect or are likely to receive more official appointments to high office because of the election — rather, the opposite. The new President's cabinet and "official family" showed no special religious flavor, and ambassadorial and other appointments have been without religious significance. The most prominent Catholics in government continue to be those in the Congress, where their position is independent of executive action and often enough at odds with administrative policy.

The effect of the 1960 election on the Church as an institution in American life is difficult to predict. Almost any visible change in the relation of the Church to the government would be cause for public comment and reaction; a new friendliness would be interpreted as a "take-over," coolness would be attributed to clerical dissatisfaction with the autonomy of the President. Whatever influence the Church might have had in public policy in times past, and however it may have been exercised, a Catholic President would be likely, if only for political reasons, to show himself independent of the clergy. This attitude has already been manifested in the controversial school aid issue, and we can expect further examples of it.

Another important effect of the election on Catholics will be an increased emphasis on the role of the layman in the life of the Church in America. This will be subtle but certain. All over the world, expansion of the role of the layman is a present concern of the bishops. New ways and means must be found to draw the lay Catholic more profoundly into the daily life and operations of the Church. In keeping with the American political tradition, the Catholic clergy were reluctant to involve themselves in the campaign of 1960. This attitude gave a wide opportunity to American Catholic laymen to be heard on religious questions and to take the forefront in interpreting the Church to the community. On religious questions during the campaign, the Catholic candidate sought the assistance not of clerics but rather of well-informed lay people who might guide him in interpreting Catholic teaching for the American public. There was no need to consult clerical sources, since the kind of religious information that was most important during the campaign was easily available from informed Catholic lay persons. The famous speech at Houston, Texas, delivered before a group of rather hostile ministers of religion, indicated a firm grasp of the Catholic position and a clear understanding of the competing autonomies of religion and politics. There was no evidence that assistance in its preparation had come from any but lay Catholic sources.

Foreign observers have often suggested that the paucity of lay leadership among American Catholics can be attributed to the lack of a Catholic aristocratic tradition in our country. There is a sense in which this appears to be true, especially when we observe in England and on the Continent the leadership in Church affairs exercised by the "old Catholic families" who claim a kind of hereditary "right to be heard" in ecclesiastical matters. If this is the case, the election of a Catholic President probably comes as close to establishing such a social class as is possible in our country. Wealth and even power are not sufficient in themselves; there must be the public prestige which the presidential office, successfully administered, would seem to bring. Even if this is an exaggerated explanation when taken alone, it is certain that the most prominent layman in the American Church is bound to be the President while in office, and this example and symbol will emphasize the importance of lay leadership and the possibilities it offers for the mission of the Church. In support of it an emerging group of highly qualified lay leaders on several levels is already discernible. The statement on the relation between religion and politics signed by one hundred sixty-two Catholic intellectuals and circulated during the election campaign was a significant phenomenon. The statement was planned and composed entirely by laymen; no members of the hierarchy or persons in ecclesiastical status were involved even for its approval. Without offending the teaching authority of the Church, this lay group undertook an action having considerable public influence entirely on its own. Such an effort in an earlier era would have been interpreted as hostility toward proper Church authorities, or even been impossible.

Finally, a realistic view of the campaign must convince Catholics of the necessity of a continued and expanded dialogue with their neighbors of other religions. Those Protestant voices that were raised so quickly in defense of Catholics when they were assaulted by other Protestant elements were precisely the voices which had been heard over the preceding decade in open and friendly dialogue with Catholics. It was no mere happenstance that the people who understood the Catholic Church best were those who had participated in amicable social and intellectual interchange with Catholics. It is also plain that the areas in which bitterness and misunderstanding were most prominent were also the areas where contact was minimal or nonexistent. No one would suggest that the dialogue will dissolve all differences; this would please no one. But what the dialogue can do is to open new areas of mutual understanding, so that differences do not any longer form barriers with social and political consequences but become merely boundaries indicating the extent of confirmed religious commitments.

Each religious tradition considers its fundamental tenets important and does not intend to compromise them. At the same time, experience indicates that a vast amount of misinformation and misinterpretation still circulates. The separate religious communities simply do not know each other well enough to build that common confidence which the good society requires. The dialogue has given an opportunity for face-to-face discussion in an atmosphere of candor and friendliness. The campaign demonstrated the effectiveness of this dialogue on many levels, and old prejudices on both sides were at least partly dissolved by calm and sympathetic appraisals publicly presented on appropriate occasions. To be sure, only a beginning has been made, but the line of action has been set.

The presidential campaign of 1960 was a transforming experience for both Catholics and Protestants. How lasting its good effects will be depends upon how wisely our citizens use what has been accomplished through it. One thing is sure; the campaign was a unique opportunity which will not be offered again. History will label only John F. Kennedy as the "first President of the United States who was a Catholic." Yet even if we fail to take advantage of the further special opportunities his election offered for an improvement of the pluralistic religious relationships in the United States — and this would indeed be regrettable — we should acknowledge that certain gains have already been realized, more promising than anyone could have foreseen.

6

The Church and the Image

MANY people may wonder why there should be any anxiety over the image that the Church presents to the public at large. Is it, after all, important for the mission of the Church, for its work in the world, to *appear* to be what it actually is, or is it enough that the Church *is* its true self? Has not Madison Avenue influenced the thinking of those who worry over what image of the Church is in the popular mind?

Even if the terminology is new, the concept is not, for it has always been important to know in what way the Church has projected itself as a contemporary institution. It is not farfetched to say that the admonitions of the Lord himself show that he thought it a matter of some importance how people judged the Church which he was sending into the world for the salvation of all men. "By this let all men know that you are mine," he told the apostles, "that you have love one for another." (John 13:35) And "So let your light shine before men that they see the glory of Our Father who is in heaven." (Matt. 5:16)

While the history of the Church affords examples of considerable damage to its public image through human failure, Church regulations from the earliest days have been concerned with the impression its institutional life makes on the general community. If the Church is truly the extension of Christ in the world, it has the responsibility to present to mankind an unmistakable resemblance to Christ. This surely is one explanation of the elaborate Church law which regulates its external life and the official actions of those who make up its formal ecclesiastical structure.

Catholics have no need to research an image of the Church in order to be certain that the Church is being presented authentically in every context. Such a pattern already exists. For Catholics the Church is the Mystical Body of which Christ is the Head; it is Christ still in the world, teaching, ruling, and sanctifying men. Therefore, it should reflect in every historic situation those qualities and characteristics with which Scripture and Tradition have surrounded the person of Christ. From the long-established teachings of Christian doctrine it is possible to draw the characteristics of the Church very specifically. Catholics maintain that the Church can be identified by certain "marks" which set it apart from all other institutions and that these marks are the badge of its genuine character. Traditionally, the marks are four: The Church is one, holy, catholic, and apostolic. In the next chapter, we shall discuss these characteristics in detail.

In preparation for the Second Vatican Council, Pope John spoke several times on the matter of the image of the Church. "Everything that the new Ecumenical Council is to do," said the Pontiff, "is really aimed at restoring to full splendor the simple and pure lines that the face of the Church of Jesus had at its birth, and at presenting it as its Divine Founder made it." The aim of the Council, in his words again, "is to pause a little in a loving study of the Church and try to rediscover the lines of her more fervent youth and to reconstruct them in a way that will reveal their power over modern minds." The Pope's concern is heightened by his interest in opening new avenues of understanding with those who are not Catholic and in promoting Church unity.

The Church has never consciously adopted modern public relations techniques in order to project its authentic image to the public at any precise moment. The popular image during the nineteenth century, for example, and the first half of this century in the United States was anything but a conscious projection of the Church in the American community. On the contrary, it was an accumulation of the most obvious and least lovely features visible from outside the Church at that moment. Normally, any institution responds to the pressing claims of its essential purpose before attending to those not demanding immediate action. Until recent years, the Catholic Church in the United States, as we have explained, had the formidable task of keeping the faith of millions of immigrant people as they adapted themselves to the American way of life. With this came the added burden of building up, from very small resources, the total institutional life of the Catholic Church in America. Church leadership during this period was made up largely of men gifted with administrative ability, who could meet the challenges in organization and expansion. That work in many parts of our country is far from complete even now, but the Church can turn some of its attention to questions which at an earlier time would have been considered secondary.

Certainly the time is propitious for thinking out the implications of the image of the Catholic Church in America, now that the older view has been effectively shattered. It would be absurd to suggest that no one in America will ever again think of the Catholic Church in terms of the earlier caricature. Undoubtedly, the older generation of Americans will retain some trace of this deeply incised image in spite of contradicting evidence. The rising generation, however, will find it impossible to accept the hoary caricature as meeting the realities they experience when they confront the Catholic Church in its American context. They will make from new material a new image, which, in its broad lines, will probably also be the image for the following generation.

One may ask what resources are at hand to assist the Church in presenting a new and more favorable image on the American scene. Is the Church better situated as an institution for presenting its authentic face to the public than it was a generation ago? In the formation of the new image, who will make the largest contribution and in what manner? Where are the most likely allies in this endeavor?

It is proper that the official position which the Church takes on contemporary issues should set the pattern for its public image. The official leaders of the Church, those who represent its teaching authority, have the right to speak in its name and express its present aims in the life of the community, and the public should expect them to do so. In this sense the hierarchy, especially in their public statements, will always draw the broad lines by which the Church is judged in the mind of the whole society. Theirs is the authentic voice of Christ speaking among men, and it is to the living authority of the Church that men must look for that divine guidance which the Lord himself promised. Thus, the pronouncements of the hierarchy, taken together, provide the broad outlines of the image of the Church which our neighbors should accept as authentic, because it is the one which Catholics themselves accept and by which their lives and actions are directed.

In addition, the view people will have of the Church will be colored by a vast number of auxiliary factors which fill in, widen, and interpret what the official voice of the Church has unmistakably presented. Although secondary and unofficial, they are highly important because they interpret in the language of the marketplace what the teaching authority of the Church has outlined in theological or moral terms. First of these is the Catholic press, whose function it is to present to the Catholic people of America and their neighbors the day-to-day life of the Church and the present implications of Catholic teaching in their lives. Except in those rare instances in which members of the hierarchy speak officially in its pages, the Catholic press has no share in the teaching authority of the Church. On the other hand, its function is most important, because it translates into current and local terms the familiar principles and the long-standing directives of the official Church authority.

The Catholic press in the United States has achieved the maturity to engage in self-analysis and to admit that several points of view may be applicable to a single situation. Like the other special institutions within the Church in years gone by, the press reflected the hostile social climate, and in its pages one often found partisan pleading and a narrowness of interest which seemed to exclude the needs and demands of the wider community. Today the press mirrors the general maturity and sophistication of the Catholic population. Readers feel themselves persuaded rather than commanded, and publishers expect varied reactions rather than docile acceptance when they take a stand on debatable issues.

Papers of high quality are flourishing in the Catholic community, and are a sign of willingness to accept responsibility for the intellectual position of the Church in the

American community. The last ten years have seen a new kind of journalism, directed mostly by skilled Catholic laymen who have chosen a career in the service of the Church through the apostolate of the press. The loyalty of this type of journalist to the Church is beyond question, and he enjoys in increasing measure the confidence of his publisher, who is generally a member of the hierarchy. Understandably, then, lay journalists will be an increasingly important force in interpreting the Church to American Catholics and their neighbors.

Another group whose influence in the life of the Church is already large but destined to become much larger is composed of the scholars and research people in our colleges and universities. In recent years these men and women have come forward and dedicated themselves to the intellectual apostolate, most often in the field of history, philosophy, or social science. Their number is increasing and likewise their importance in the Catholic community. Much of their wide influence has come through their publications, and we have had over the last decade an extraordinary flowering of influential volumes.

In this connection the field of religious sociology is especially important since it has studied certain aspects of Church life in a scientific manner and tested the ancient ways against the new science and the social problems characteristic of our times. The Bible scholars are another notable group; in an area of special sensitivity, they have given a conspicuous example of scrupulous scientific endeavor combined with an exemplary devotion to the Church and her needs. We have no way of measuring what effect these scholars are having on their students and, in this sense, on the image of the Church among youthful Catholics. But we do know that the mind of the Catholic intellectuals of tomorrow is being soundly formed in our universities and colleges, and it is likely that their influence will be far-reaching.

Another group is difficult to categorize but in general we may speak of them as Catholics in public life. The President himself, willy-nilly, leads this group in presenting the image of the Church. Since he has the distinction of being the Chief Executive of the United States, people will think first of him when they think of Catholics in public life. His responsibilities in this matter will be shared by the Catholics in the Cabinet, in the Congress, and in the Supreme Court, and also by all others who hold a prominent commission in our national or state governments.

Fidelity in attending Church services and frequent appearances at Catholic functions will contribute less to the formation of a favorable image of the Church than the picture of the dedicated public servant who carries out his duties without partisan emphasis or appearance of special interest. Americans are seeing less and less of the old-time politician familiar to the immigrant. In his stead are appearing men of fine character and education as well as good will whose devotion to their country and fidelity in the pursuit of its interest must awaken the respect of all who observe them in their official actions. There will be Catholics among such men. The old image of the conniving politician will not be dissipated at once, nor will its connection with the immigrant be immediately forgotten. As in the past, what Catholic men in public office do and say, and even in some measure their conduct in their personal lives, will have enormous influence on what their fellow citizens think of the Catholic Church. Like every other institution, the Church will be judged by its fruits, and the most obvious are Catholic men in the public view.

A factor which must be mentioned more because of its potential influence than its present importance is the Catholic pulpit. There are many problems connected with preaching in a Catholic pulpit, some of which are not at all appreciated by those outside the Church or by some in it. Catholic sermons are usually delivered in connection with the Mass; as a result they must be brief, taking not more than ten or fifteen minutes. In content they are adequate but uninspired. This is understandable. The congregations in most parishes reflect a wide variety of background and education, quite in contrast with the often socially stratified Protestant denominations. For the most part, preachers find a lowest common denominator, or at best a median, and then preach at that level. The result often satisfies neither the congregation nor the preacher. With the new interest in homiletics and with better training in the seminaries we may expect the situation to improve in the years ahead. If it does, the pulpits of America will make a very effective contribution to the changing image of the Church. They will be speaking almost exclusively to Catholics, but those Catholics in turn, in moving through the community, will reflect the more precise image they themselves have acquired from the pulpit. This is an opportunity which has not yet been exploited to any advantage but offers rich opportunities.

An institution as large as the Catholic Church does not have to present itself consciously to the community in order to make an impression; its very size and activity provide some kind of picture. The grave risk of making no effort to present the authentic image is that a distorted one will develop, as in the past, and again the Church will be judged by its often unlovely or merely human external qualities rather than those divine characteristics which give it its authentic claim on the minds of men.

For all these reasons, then, the Catholic Church in the United States now faces the critical matter of a new image. Certainly the situation is not parallel with that of a large business or commercial enterprise eager to make the proper impression on the public. The Church emphatically is not just one other institution of a community; it has a unique place and a unique message. All the same, the Church can profit by the various techniques of presentation and persuasion which a deeper understanding of human psychology has produced in this century. This is no more than being a part of contemporary life. The more social forces it can put to apostolic use, the more successfully will its divine message be spread and accepted. The Church through all the centuries has shown a willingness to adapt itself to new things — witness, in our time, religion's use of radio and television for reaching a wider public in an effective way. The science of sociology and its related arts, of which public relations is one, are offering new insights which might also be used to advantage. The techniques of public relations appear to be falling on bad days because they have sometimes been put to dishonest use. This is likely to cause good men to consider it improper that the life of the Church should be involved in any operation which looks so much like manipulation. Such an attitude misses a point which is of paramount importance; *abusus rei usum non tollit* — the abuse of an element does not argue against its use, the scholastics used to say.

Facts of social existence which are often debased for crass and commercial use can also be elevated and put to the service of great and noble causes; in this manner the social facts, in a sense, can be made to redeem themselves. The image we have been urging is not to be a false image, not a portrait drawn in flattering lines; but rather the *authentic* image of the Church, that total view which includes in proper proportion the divine and the human and makes both of these visible to the contemporary world. Under no circumstances should the Catholic Church set up a kind of bureau of public relations which would attempt to make certain that on every possible occasion the image of the Church would somehow correspond with some master image at a central ecclesiastical headquarters. This would itself be a distortion, as well as a kind of humbug on the public. In point of fact, it would not even be effective, for the American public is not taken in by every attempt at persuasion, and it can see through fradulent techniques to the heart of the matter. The vast sums of money so often spent on the projection of a public image for people and institutions are money wasted, because the superficial character of these images is so evident; the observer, instead of being impressed, is turned away by an obvious deception.

What is important is that the Church — Church leadership and laity — be aware that there is in formation a public image of the Catholic Church, and that the large dimension of this image can even now be distorted. For example, the size of the Catholic Church in America — roughly one-fifth of the population — can seem formidable to non-Catholics. Latent fear can readily transform size into power in the public view unless it is evident that this solidarity is a religious and spiritual thing, beyond political or economic or social manipulations.

It will be important, especially as the Church grows in size and influence in the life of America, to make it plain again and again that Catholics are united to the papacy in a spiritual allegiance which leaves them free to accept a thousand lesser loyalties on all levels of American life. If Catholics are conscious that their neighbors can misunderstand, even with the best of intentions, what is said and done by the Church on the American scene, they will make what extra effort is required to translate present realities and intentions for the future into understandable terms for the rest of the community. This minimal awareness is all that is required to present the Church to the American public in terms that will be comprehensible and acceptable.

If the image of the Church at every moment in its history is in harmony with its traditional marks — if the Church is seen to be one, holy, catholic, and apostolic — those outside the Church will have an authentic picture. This gives the clue to the kind of image that must be projected in the years ahead; it must be one that responds faithfully to these traditional features. Where these qualities are visible in the public image of the Catholic Church, and visible in their traditional meaning, there its neighbors will see the Church as it was established, and recognize, as much as faith allows, the character of the Church founded by Christ.

7

The New Look

THE REMAKING of the image of the Catholic Church in America should focus not upon its size or its power, its social composition or its accomplishments, but on those essential qualities — its "marks" — which identify it in every generation. Although these are spiritual qualities, they are recognizable through their manifestations. A Church that is *one* is preoccupied with unity, a Church that is *holy* finds its strength in a solid sanctity, a Church that is *catholic* embraces men without discrimination, and a Church that is *apostolic* drinks deeply of the revelation given to the apostles. These marks, then, are the attributes which should characterize any image which lays claim to authenticity.

It will be profitable to review these traditional attributes and to attempt to relate them to the contemporary American scene, with a view to dispelling some difficulties for non-Catholics.

If the marks are the characterizing features of the

Church, why are they not immediately evident to all wherever the Church exists and works? For the convinced Catholic, this does not present a problem of any proportions. He knows that the Church is larger than any Catholic or group of Catholics. For him, the Church exists primarily as the Body of Christ, and just as the Lord's body, when he was on earth, was afflicted and abused, so too his Mystical Body, the Church, does not exist in this world in a risen, glorified state but is on its way to becoming, in the words of the Scripture, "the spotless bride." For this reason the marks of the Church exist truly but imperfectly, and it is the task of all members of the Body to bring it closer to final perfection. Thus the Church was Catholic in promise and mission at the time of the Lord, whereas in our time it is Catholic, or universal, in fact as well, in the sense that it is world-wide, though it has not yet been brought to all individuals. The constitution and commitment of the Church are unchanging, but the realization of its promise under God's providence is accomplished in time.

The first distinguishing characteristic of the Catholic Church, then, and the first impression its image should give, is its unity. Catholics and most other Christians through the centuries have believed that Christ intended his Church to be one: "Thou art Peter and upon this rock I will build my Church." (Matt. 16:18) It is the teaching of the Catholic Church, and also of the Anglican and

Eastern Orthodox Churches, that the unity of the institution Christ established to serve all men as the proper and ordained road to salvation is a visible as well as a spiritual unity. Certain Protestant churches also share this general view, although with variant interpretations.

The visible unity of the Catholic Church — the unity of a single authority, the unity of faith and practice — is commonly recognized by the most casual observer. It is widely known that all Catholics living in a certain area accept the authority of the local bishop, who is appointed to office by the visible head of the Church, the Pope. It is plain also that all Catholics receive the same sacraments and accept the same truths in matters of faith and morals. People of broad experience, moreover, know that the Catholic Church in all parts of the world takes on local colorations, that it preaches and teaches in native languages, assumes local customs and in many ways adapts itself to the customs of different peoples. At the same time, underneath this diversity they see a singleness of commitment and belief. So clear, in fact, is the basic and lasting unity of the institution they know as the Catholic Church that it strikes some of them as a rigid conformity almost incompatible with man's freedom of conscience.

It would appear, then, that Catholics in America as elsewhere, when they show themselves so truly one, at least give an opportunity to their neighbors to see in them one of the distinguishing marks of the Church of Christ. Is not this enough? Is this not being as Catholic as is necessary?

Actually, it is only a beginning. When Catholics are satisfied with this degree of unity, they are not being *totally* faithful to the prayer of Christ. The Lord prayed that *"all* may be one as thou, Father, in me and I in thee." (John 17:21) This does not mean merely unity with those who are already a part of the Catholic Church, but unity with all who claim the name Christian and with all those to whom the gospel can be preached. The Lord sought a single unity by which all men would find salvation, and that unity was his Church.

Consequently, Catholics must concern themselves with the problem of Christian unity in its widest aspects — with what today is known as ecumenism. The Catholic position seems the simplest possible and is often described in uncompromising language. Christ founded a single Church, the Catholic Church, and in the course of time the weakness of men brought about a long series of historic divisions which shattered its pristine unity. The Church's task ever since has been to restore what was lost by bringing back those who have wandered from the oneness that Christ established. Seeing the picture thus simply and clearly, what is there for Catholics to do but to ask their Christian neighbors to set aside the differences, acknowledge the accretions and losses which the years have multiplied, and return in submission to that common fold which the Good Shepherd himself established? Put in these terms, the claims of the Catholic Church seem hard and uncompromising, not at all suited to the beginnings of anything like a dialogue in ecumenism.

Are Christians then so far apart, so irreconcilably separated in view, that ecumenism for Catholics can mean nothing more than marking time, waiting for others to come to their senses? Or does it afford an opportunity for Catholics to present to their Christian neighbors the various claims of the Church, to interpret them, and finally persuade other Christians of their validity?

When the lines are drawn so sharply, ecumenism becomes a subject which must be treated in terms of centuries and not of years. Just as the fracturing of Christian unity was the product of a long history, so the return to Christian unity will require many years for its final success. In the meantime Catholics must be ready to sit down in charity with all who sincerely seek to serve Christ and to be part of his Church; they must take part in a common work to remove layer after layer of historic accumulations of divisive elements and lay bare the spiritual essentials behind them. Together we must study the Scriptures and Christian Tradition with patience and with mutual trust, so that out of our common studies will come forth the unmistakable voice and character of Christ himself. When, in this connection, charged words like "submission" are used, there is bound to be misunderstanding among those whose frame of reference for historic reasons is different from the Catholic's.

Under no circumstances should the unity of the Church be thought of as demanding uniformity. Nothing will cause the contemporary American to shy away from the claims of religion more than the suggestion that he must abdicate his rightful independence as a person. With the mounting pressures moving men toward conformity in so many areas, it is important to emphasize that the unity of the Church is not a conformity which destroys man's proper spiritual autonomy. Unity in the Church is a deeper acceptance of transcendental realities which, essentially lasting and unchanging, in different eras and places find different external expressions. A glance at the Catholic Church through the centuries should convince us that nothing resembling conformity could express its essential unity. Within the Church there is, for example, an immense variety of rites or modes of worship — ranging from the ancient Byzantine and Armenian to the Latin or Roman rite practiced by the largest number of present-day Catholics. Each is faithful to certain customs and to certain times, but each preserves as well those essentials of Christian belief and worship without which the Church could not be called Catholic.

In our strivings for Christian unity certain customary forms of expression and certain formulations of doctrine may not receive immediate acceptance from those outside the Catholic Church. The centuries-old division can be bridged only by patient effort and understanding and by a willingness on all sides to translate into contemporary language ancient and long-accepted concepts. Pope Leo XIII reminded us the principal aim is not merely to build or to organize a Christian Church in which all may be happily one; what is being sought is the unity which Christ himself has already set in his Church. Unity does not consist in making anything new. It comes by discovering something already existent, though to some not yet evident.

believe that the Lord plainly made his
oblem together is to discover, with the
here that unity now lies.

, Catholics come to the discussion of
al honesty. They know in their hearts
the insight of faith, where the unity
those who do not know, they must be
patient guides, accepting the sincerity of their searching and offering them the enlightenment God has given through faith. No man can be forced into Christ's Church; he comes willingly and by his own acceptance, and he comes ultimately by the inspiration of God's grace. The task here as elsewhere is to become instruments of God working in time to achieve that universal Christian unity which was the clear mark of the Church Christ established. But if Catholics in America do not interest themselves in dialogue and ecumenism, if they avoid stretching out their hands to those Christians and others who are clearly searching for unity, how can they be said to be fulfilling the historic and divine desire "that all may be one"?

Again we can see reasons why Catholics tend to be uninterested in the religious activities of their Protestant neighbors. A generation and more ago this was inevitable; it was a time when Catholics were a struggling minority and most Protestant leaders were unfriendly. Moreover any overture, by Protestant and Catholic alike, was likely to be regarded as an attempt at proselytism or at best a fruitless venture in religious communication. The present context has altered all this. The highest leadership in many Protestant areas is eager for new understanding, and Catholics have acquired an appreciation of American history which should banish shyness, fear, and isolation. The very constitution of the Catholic faith, the first mark of the Church, requires a contemporary effort for unity under contemporary conditions.

We turn now to a second quality or mark of the Church: the Church is holy. By that it is meant that the Church is holy in its founder, holy as a Church, and produces Christians of eminent holiness. The work of the Holy Spirit whom the Lord sent after his Ascension was a work of sanctification; he came to make men holy. This describes in a single phrase the basic function of the Church in the world. Léon Bloy was fond of remarking that "our task is to make saints." It is through the distribution of divine grace that God uses the Church to make men holy. The sacramental life of man which begins with Baptism is a growth in holiness. We say in Baptism that a person is "christened." This ancient religious word means that he is made into another Christ, that he puts on Christ and begins in his own life the life of Christ.

Observers outside the Church admit that among those who claim the name Catholic there are recognizable numbers of very holy people. It is at least as plain that there are large numbers of sinners. If we may speak of the Church as a Church of saints, we must also acknowledge that it is a Church of sinners. What does this say about the basic holiness of the Church? Since man is free, he is able, by his own decision, to cooperate with the grace of God and take the road that leads to glory, or to refuse this cooperation and take the road that leads to shame. The Church comes to the Christian's assistance, offering advice, aid, and encouragement to the good life, but the Church never is able to force goodness upon him. For those who do cooperate with God's grace, sanctity is the highest Christian experience and a begining of that final union with God which will be known only in eternal life.

The Catholic Church over the years has inspired to high sanctity those heroes of the Christian life who are called saints. These are the ones who have turned their back upon the world and upon self and in a dedication inspired by the love of God have given themselves totally to others. Perhaps it is more accurate to say that they have seen the world, and their own place in it, as an opportunity to work for God in a special way among men. Sometimes this means a life of action and sometimes a life of contemplation; sometimes it means a life in the world and sometimes a life withdrawn from the world; but it is always a life given away in the name of the Lord himself.

Spectacular examples of sanctity, because they are more dramatic, are apt to be more impressive and to attract wider attention than the ordinary forms which we encounter in daily life. Moreover, the human character turns in wonder to the curious and to the different. The Lord intended that uncommon gifts should mark those who were called to special sanctity, and his own life was surrounded by marvels intended to draw men to God. He promised, moreover, that such marvels would be one of the signs of those who would speak in his name. "And these signs shall attend those who believe; in my name they shall cast out devils; they shall speak in new tongues; they shall take up serpents; and if they drink any deadly thing, it shall not hurt them; they shall lay hands upon the sick and they shall get well." (Mark 16:17)

By a curious turn of human history, it is that element which is most clearly Scriptural, most evident in the life of the Master himself and those who immediately followed him in the life of the Church, which in our time tends to frighten away the unbeliever and cause him to hold the Christian Church in disrepute. People often speak of the "wonder element" in the Catholic faith and its influence in practices of Catholic piety. The extraordinary phenomenon of Lourdes, for example, is thought by many to be an example of Catholic credulity and something very close to superstition. The various other apparitions of Mary, and

the strange tales that are told of certain saints, are all likely
to dismay the modern who expects to find in Christian
teaching merely the principles of the Golden Rule and the
acknowledgment of the God of love and mercy. Yet
similar phenomena in apostolic days were historically the
earliest signs by which men were drawn to the Christian
faith. Few things are more evident than the fact that
Christ intended that his Church should, in the working
of time, be one full of wonder and that these very wonders
should stir faith in men's hearts.

There is, however, a distinction between those practices
of piety which the Catholic Church allows and those
essential signs of holiness which, if we may use the phrase,
are the "machinery of sanctification." It is not proper to
equate certain pietistic practices with the essential sacramental life of the Church. By God's design, at every crucial
moment in human existence there is a special sacrament
to pour into the human soul new resources of divine grace
on which the Christian may draw for strength and inspiration in its quest for ever more complete union with Him.
For the Catholic, Baptism begins the Christian life in the
soul, and subsequently the six other sacraments — in time
of youth and of age, in health and in illness — come to the
support of weak humanity and make it possible to maintain
and deepen friendship with God. Of special importance is
the sacrament of Christ's own Body and Blood, the Eucharist, by which the Catholic receives into his own person
the Body, Blood, Soul, and Divinity of Our Lord and

Savior, providing a new intimacy and a unique strength to the wavering soul.

It is the sacraments which are the principal source of man's holiness. One cannot place in this same category those various aids to piety which sometimes seem to be accretions on the body of the Church as it moves through time. Sometimes Catholic piety seems to be measured in terms of certain Marian devotions, well-attended novenas, the popularity of particular saints, and many other traditional Catholic practices. It is not necessary to turn one's back upon these devotions, when they are proper, but they should not be made a touchstone of religion. Their place among the means of human sanctification is not central, but peripheral. The Church stresses the Christocentric nature of salvation, and it places in proper focus the huge reality of the Redemption and the fruits of that Redemption which God placed in his Church for man's use in finding his way to salvation. At the same time, pious practices have received the blessings of the Church in every generation and are expected to emphasize the Communion of Saints and that fellowship of love which binds all followers of Christ one to another. It is also through the pious devotion to the saints that the Church Triumphant, made up of the saints in heaven, is linked in a special manner with the Church Militant, or the faithful on earth. These devotions, however popular they may be, can never take the place of the sacramental life, and Catholics do not equate the two, nor substitute one for the other.

It is easy for those unfamiliar with details of Catholic practice to misunderstand the varying emphases that the practicing Catholic places upon different pious actions. Preachers and press may often emphasize the wondrous and colorful and neglect in some measure the traditional and the unvaried. This is no indication of their relative importance in the true scheme of things. We know the attractiveness of the new, and sometimes a particular devotion appears to answer a need of the moment. But the Catholic Church, which sees fashions come and go, does not fail to call its people back to the table of the Lord when they wander away, nor fail to remind them always of the riches of divine grace which the Lord has left them in his sacraments.

The truly wondrous things in the history of Christianity are not the miracles that may have occurred here or there, nor even certain apparitions which have excited and amazed the faithful and others. The truly wondrous element in the life of the Church in every age is the presence of Christ, who continues to live mystically in his Church and to be present among his people. "I am with you all days even to the end of the world." (Matt. 28:20) This is the real wonder of Christianity, the source of its greatness and the source of its holiness. Unless we understand this, we do not see beneath the surface of Catholic practice, and we judge in a superficial way the strivings of mankind toward the kingdom of God. The holiness of the Church is the holiness of Christ, and it is from this core of sanctity that all Christian souls are made holy. "No one comes to the Father except through me." (John 14:6) These words make it plain where the heart and center of the Christian faith lies and where all men must turn if they will drink of the fountain of holiness.

How important it is that this second "mark" of the Church not merely be present but also be clearly visible to those outside the Church, and never be obscured by a preoccupation with various forms of piety and personal devotions! Contrary to some widespread misconceptions, the current interest in the liturgy of the Church is not concerned so much with the outward forms of piety as with the central fact of the Son's worship of the Father and our participation in this worship. It is in this sense that Catholics are truly Christians, for it is in Christ and through him that they direct their worship to the Father. Christ is their Head and Mediator; thus, in liturgical prayer there is a dynamic union with Christ in *his* prayer; in the Mass there is a union of mind and heart with him in *his* Sacrifice; in the Eucharist there is the highest bond of unity with *him;* and in all the sacraments there is a personal encounter with Christ that requires a living faith and an individual response.

Understandably the pressures of a divided Christianity and the necessity of apologetics in past generations tended to make indistinct some of these basic theological facts, as Catholics concentrated on defense of truths that were under assault. The new interest in the liturgy, encouraged so effectively by the Popes of the twentieth century, once again emphasizes the principle that Christian sanctification and worship, by God's own design for his Church, take place primarily in the community and through its action.

One cannot pass over, in this connection, the manner in which the Church through its moral teaching contributes to the sanctification of society and its members. Especially in modern times, when even moral principles are under heavy assault from so many quarters, the ethical teachings of the Church and its counsels of perfection direct, encourage, and inspire men to a life which, very often against the current of the moment, is essentially holy.

The third attribute traditionally mentioned is that the Church is catholic. Although the word itself was not common until the time of St. Ignatius, martyr (A.D. 107), the quality it represents was a characteristic from the beginning. The Lord's admonition to his apostles struck the note: "going therefore, make disciples of nations" (Matt. 28:19); "go into the whole world and preach the gospel to every creature." (Mark 16:15) This is the origin of the catholicity or universality of the Catholic Church. Christ plainly intended his message to be a message for all mankind, a means of salvation by which the human race would find its way to God. Nothing could be clearer than the international character of the Church, which embraces all peoples within its fold and makes no distinctions among them on the basis of color or race or origin.

In our day, the shrinking world has made it possible to comprehend even more fully than in earlier times the universal nature of the Church. The world has seen its refusal to be identified with the West against the East, or with the white against the black, or with either side in any of the distinctive quarrels which mark the present history of man on this earth. The highest ruling body of the Church, the Sacred College of Cardinals, from whose number the Pope is selected, reflects this extraordinary variety of acceptance and mission which the Church considers its own. There are cardinals from Japan, the Philippines, China, and India; cardinals from Africa as well as from the ancient Christian sees of Europe and the newer countries of the Americas. The mission effort of the Church has never restricted itself to one class of people or to one race; it has embraced all humanity, whether peoples of high civilization or tribes close to primitive life.

This broad view of both mankind and the mission of the Church has demonstrated in striking fashion the Catholic Church's belief in its own catholicity. But all of this, visible and dramatic and historic as it may be, is only the expression of an inner catholicity which lies at the center of Catholic teaching. Christ came for the salvation of the world and brought his redemptive message for all mankind. The blood that was shed on Calvary was not shed for one time or for one people; it was shed for the redemption of the human race, and all men in every age have a claim upon this redemption. This is the doctrine which makes it impossible for the doors of that Church to be closed permanently against any man, except by his own choice.

There is also another way in which the Church is catholic, and this is in its appeal to the whole man. The Catholic Church is not simply a *rational* religion nor simply a *voluntary* one; in other words, it is not one that involves only the mind or only the heart. The Church attends to and lays claim to the total man, respects and honors every aspect of his life; it inspires his mind and his body, his will and his emotions; it baptizes the entire man and so puts its mark upon his total life. This is not the same thing as saying that every act of man is a religious act or that every act is one with moral or ethical implications. But when a man "puts on Christ," and in this act becomes a Christian, all his conscious activities are from that moment given a new inspiration and a new responsibility.

Those who observe the Church from outside cannot fail to note a striking social phenomenon about which Catholics themselves often speak. Since Protestant Churches are more likely to be socially stratified, it is a conspicuous feature of the Catholic Church that people of disparate station usually worship together, receive the same sacraments, listen to the same sermons, and find consolation in administrations of the same sacred functions. There are a few "fashionable" churches, and some far from fashionable, but usually anyone who worships in a Catholic church runs the risk of finding himself kneeling at the side of someone with whom he has no more in common than a single faith and a single humanity.

But is there not an extraordinary blight upon the Catholic image at the moment, which Catholics have not done their share to remove? Racial injustice continues to mark the American society on many levels, and Catholics are part of the society which permits it to continue. The American Negro has not until recently provided much of a problem nor a very serious challenge to the Catholic Church in the United States. The majority of Negroes were brought to our country by Protestants, and they settled in a part of America in which Catholics are still only a small minority. There were exceptions, of course; Louisiana, with its French traditions, is one, and Maryland, with its English Catholic past, another. For the most part, however, in the years before and after the Civil War the preponderance of American Negroes have been under Protestant influence and have been members of Protestant denominations, notably the Baptist and Methodist. In addition, the years after the Civil War were years in which Catholics themselves were suffering from certain serious disabilities and trying to adjust their own social situation in an unfriendly environment. Thus there is some excuse for those decades in which the American Catholic Church said little about racial injustice.

During recent years, however, things have been different. Catholic leadership on a high level has expressed itself again and again in favor of social justice for all citizens, and it has also described the serious social implications of Church teaching on race relations. Some of the Catholic bishops in the South, presiding over very small dioceses, have been among the first to call to public attention the injustice of discrimination and segregation. No one is likely to forget the extraordinary situation in New Orleans that obliged Archbishop Rummel in 1959 to excommunicate members of his flock who refused to receive in their parish a colored priest assigned to them. In 1962 the Archbishop announced the immediate integration of Catholic schools for the fall term and was publicly scolded by a vocal minority of Catholics who were later excommunicated. Other incidents of the same nature have occurred elsewhere, and the Negro in America at the present time is likely to consider the Catholic Church one of his staunchest allies in his plea for social equality.

The integration of Catholic schools in the border states and in the North has been swift and impressive. All the same, a close study of the picture is not a happy one from every point of view. There have been areas in the South where Church leadership has declined to speak even in moments of crisis, and there have been occasions when those who were spokesmen for the Church spoke with an ambiguity that was interpreted as pusillanimity. At a time which seems to call for bold and dramatic action, there has been considerably less action than some elements among the Negroes feel they had a right to expect.

Justice for the Negro is by no means a problem only for

the South. The problem is more pressing in the North than in the South and larger in the urban centers of America than in the countryside. The majority of Catholics, of course, are situated in and around the great cities of our country. In the last two decades the mobility of the Negro population has increased tremendously, and vast migrations from the South have brought colored families into many of the large northern cities. Like the white immigrants before them, they have moved into the less desirable sections of the city, which have been promptly abandoned by the whites. They have been forced to live in ghettos and pay high rents for the most unhealthy kind of substandard dwellings. The problem worsens when the Negro is in a position, in terms of both education and finance, to move into the suburban American community. Here the chasm is inevitably reached, and the middle-class American Negro faces the most serious impasse of all. He must move out of the slum tenements to bring up his children in the free air and sunshine of America, but once out he encounters not merely talk and insult, but even physical assault and violence.

In the expanding suburbs which surround the great cities there are concentrations of Catholics whose record in this matter leaves something to be desired. For many years Catholic Interracial Councils have been in existence — small groups of people dedicated to promoting interracial justice. Only within the last two years, however, have these struggling and almost ineffective groups been brought together to form a National Conference on Interracial Justice. Of course, there have been heroes working in this field. The venerable names of Father John LaFarge and Mother Katherine Drexel, both from old American families, will be held in benediction for many generations for the work they have accomplished among the Negroes of America. There are many others who should share a place with these. Religious orders of men and women, like the Josephite Fathers and the Society of the Divine Word, have made their special apostolate the work among the Negroes, and their efforts are responsible in some measure for the present good will among Negroes toward the Catholic Church. But the average urban American Catholic is not yet aware of his responsibilities as a member of a Church that does not allow distinction among peoples. Many Catholics who stand in the way of racial justice in housing and employment do so without being aware that in these acts they betray their faith and damage the true image of the Catholic Church. Many religious institutions do not yet admit qualified Negroes, and it is only within the last few years that some religious orders of men and women have accepted colored and white applicants for the religious life without differentiation. If non-Catholics, especially the Negro, fail to see the true catholicity of the Church in America, the actions of Catholics provide some of the reasons.

The relationship of Catholic and Jew in the United States is of interest in connection with this quality of catholicity.

The large confrontation of these two groups had to wait until this century, although they were immigrants together for some decades in the nineteenth century. The normal rivalry of immigrant groups existed in earliest times, but since their competition was likely to be in different areas of the economy, Jews and Catholics developed a sympathy which probably grew out of their shared minority status. Even their rising affluence tended to coincide, and they moved to the suburbs almost simultaneously.

The association of many prominent Jews with the "liberal" movements of the thirties, and with what were judged to be "left-wing" affairs generally, had some effect in alienating Catholics. Some of this antipathy still remains, but the dread experience of the Nazi pogroms stirred the Christian conscience throughout the world and an abundance of sympathy — often too self-conscious to be expressed — went out to the Jew in his suffering.

The papal leadership in this area is especially compelling. Pope Pius XI used the phrase "we are all spiritually Semites" in condemning Nazi racial theories, and his successor, Pius XII, had an almost legendary history of aid to Jewish refugees during the war, even offering asylum in the Vatican itself. Pope John, who so dramatically transformed certain liturgical expressions which could have been interpreted offensively, intervened for the lives of members of the Jewish community many times when he was papal nuncio in Budapest.

All this has had its effect in forming the minds of Catholics, and it is not strange that anti-Semitism, even among those whose older national traditions may have included this feeling, is either negligible or nonexistent. Catholics do not exclude the Jews from their missionary endeavors even though conversions among them are rare. The mission of the Church has a special interest in the *gens electa* — the Chosen People — and there are always study and prayer directed to their salvation. There are religious orders especially dedicated to this work, and the recently formed Institute of Judaeo-Christian Studies at Seton Hall College in New Jersey has already published several volumes of papers by both Christian and Jewish scholars under the meaningful title of *The Bridge,* in its effort to further understanding between the two groups. Whatever may be the attitude of the Jew during this period of religious ferment within his own religious tradition, the Catholic Church and particularly the Catholic in America does not in any way exclude him from the call of the apostolate which had such rich beginnings among his own people.

The fourth mark of the Church is its apostolic character. Catholics are fond of reminding their neighbors that the historical continuity of the Church extends back through all the centuries to the apostles, who received the commission to preach the gospel direct from the Savior. At the same time, many non-Catholics may have reason to think that their Catholic friends are not very well informed about the Scriptures and especially the New Testament, which describes these apostolic origins. It is an odd paradox that the Protestant emphasis on the primacy of the Scriptures has had the effect of alienating many Catholics from a proper familiarity with the Bible. In spite of the Church's encouragement of the reading of the Scriptures, until recently it was rarely included among the pious practices of the majority of Catholics. There was formerly a widespread notion among Protestants that Catholics did not favor the reading of the Bible and were in fact forbidden to indulge in such a devotion. Stories of chained Bibles in the Middle Ages and claims that the Bible had to wait until Protestant times to be translated into the vernacular languages all seemed to confirm this belief. Fortunately, this impression has been thoroughly dissipated. Since the establishment of the Pontifical Biblical Commission and the issuance of the great encyclical by Pope Leo XIII on Scripture studies, there can be no question concerning Catholic interest in and devotion to the sacred writings. In the Biblical field especially, Catholic scholars work in friendliest relations with Protestant scholars, as in the study of the Dead Sea Scrolls, making the point that their studies are not undertaken to promote sectarian advantage but in search of scientific truth.

The studies in ecclesiastical history which have presented the findings of the latest scientific research tend to confirm the claims of the Church to its apostolic succession. The acrimony that existed in Reformation days, and the unhappy legacy which it left behind on both sides, are now being dissolved by the careful studies of modern scholars.

Certain Catholic historians in times past tended to exaggerate for apologetic reasons; independent scholarship in which Catholics and Protestants work together has no such bias. In this connection the archaeological discoveries in Rome itself, especially those surrounding the discovery of the tomb of St. Peter, have a special interest.

The importance of the apostolic character of the Church is basic. A Church that lays claim to being the true Church founded by Christ must be able to demonstrate convincingly a valid historic continuity with the earliest Christian experience, the time of the apostles and indeed the Lord himself. With the present advances in scientific history it is no longer difficult to examine the long history of the Church and its connections with Christian beginnings. What is more difficult — and the effort has been neglected — is to demonstrate, in the midst of all the riches of the contemporary Church, those golden virtues which are specifically evangelical. Many people outside the Church cannot discern in the highly institutionalized life of the Church the primitive simplicity which marks the gospels and the apostolic Church. The experience of two thousand years and the expansion of the Church from its beginnings in Palestine required vast change and adaptation. It has been the responsibility of Christians in all ages to show that these developments and accretions need not in any essential way destroy or even submerge those special gifts and qualities which the Lord himself placed in his infant Church.

It is understandable that the very riches of the Church

may turn away souls who seek to find in the Church of Christ precisely the same simplicity which marked his own life and language as recorded in the Scriptures. Such persons are inclined to think of the Church as a static institution, a vehicle for presenting to each generation precisely the words of the Bible and no others. Such an attitude was once the Protestant mentality with which the Church came most in contact in the United States. Unless the Church was plainly a Biblical Church, it was to this mind unfaithful to its Christian origins. The new emphasis among Protestant theologians on the importance of Tradition, and on the concept of the Church as the Mystical Body of Christ, has in some measure removed this problem and prevented further misunderstanding. Among Protestant Biblical scholars there is also a new appreciation of the old fact that the Church existed before the Bible and produced it. This appreciation makes it easier for Protestants to understand the role of the Church as the conserver of Christian doctrine, the authority to which the Lord entrusted the preservation of his teaching.

For all these reasons, the claim of the Catholic Church that it is an apostolic Church is more accurately understood than it was in the past, and has become more acceptable to Protestants. The Orthodox communions in the World Council of Churches have contributed to this better understanding. Whatever else may be said about the position of the Orthodox in this extremely complex picture, the presence of Orthodox theologians at World Council discus-

sions has required of Protestants new investigation of
many basic truths of Christian doctrine which are shared
by Catholic and Orthodox alike. One more bridge of understanding has been built in this manner.

Catholics are especially sensitive to the role of Peter, as
described in the New Testament, and the primacy which he
received from the Master. Through what is called apostolic
succession, that primacy still resides in his successors. This
element in the apostolicity of the Church is much revered
among Catholics, and loyal acknowledgment of the Popes
as the successors of St. Peter has been characteristic of
Catholics in every generation. Again and again Catholics
are reminded that their Church is the Church of the apostles. While the apostolic nature of the Church is a badge
of its authenticity, it is also in the minds of believers a
singular mark of its glory. Reflection on it recalls those
spiritual heroes whom Christ gathered about him to set in
motion his way of salvation among men. An attachment to
earliest Christian origins, a preoccupation with the words
of the Lord and his life, must be visible in anyone who
claims to be Christian. Unless non-Catholics see this quality
in the image of the Catholic Church, Catholics themselves
place one more barrier between the Lord and those he came
to save.

If a pattern for an image is needed in remaking American public opinion of the Church, Catholics could not do
better than emphasize the four qualities which their most
ancient traditions supply and support. But these concepts

must be translated into a Catholic program for action — "by their fruits you shall know them." To claim the attributes without making them principles of action both for the individual Catholic and for the Church as an institution would render them sterile and meaningless. The Church that is truly and essentially one, holy, catholic, and apostolic — no matter how hostile the environment nor how frail the humanity of its members — cannot for long fail to penetrate the society in which it exists with the implications of these ideals. This has been the history of the western world.

8

The Education Issue:
A Case in Point

THE PROBLEM of Catholic education in the modern state is not found only in the United States. There are many other countries in the western world — some of long-standing Catholic tradition — where this has been a recurring problem up the present time. France, Belgium, and England come immediately to mind. The value in considering this particular problem here lies in the evidence it presents concerning the image of the Catholic Church. It is a graphic illustration of the Church in action on the American scene in a context both complex and controversial.

The basic difficulty arises where the State claims as its proper right the education of the young, and where the Church disputes this claim. Catholic teaching, strictly interpreted, allows no such right to either the State or the Church, but insists that the education of children is a right which must be exercised by parents and in whatever direction they choose for their children. However, it is also a Catholic principle that no education is complete that excludes religion. Parents are guided by the Church in this matter and fulfill their obligation by making appropriate provision for the religious upbringing of the young. Normally, this means that religion should be part of the educational curriculum from the earliest years and that it should take its place with all other branches of learning for the young.

There is nothing in this teaching that is unique to Catholics. Most Protestant groups in times gone by — and many to this day — have held similar views. An increasing number of Jewish families have also returned to this tradition. But in general there has grown up in the western world the so-called secular or state school where, in order to maintain harmony, religion is effectively excluded and the religious needs of the child are supposedly taken care of in out-of-school classes conducted by the Churches or other interested groups.

In the United States the earliest schools were religious schools, and the majority of the population when the Republic was founded believed that religion was a vital part of education. We have seen how at one time the laws in some states, such as Massachusetts, included religion as a necessary part of the public school curriculum. The Northwest Ordinance and other early laws explicitly referred to religion as a part of public education.

The hazards in this system did not become obvious until

nineteenth-century immigration began to provide a hetero-
geneous population, and Catholics, and later Jews, began to
challenge the Protestant religious teaching in the public
schools. This situation was the source of the Catholic parochial school system in America, which now includes over
five million students and, in certain large cities, educates
more than a quarter of the total student body. This exceptional and extensive school system places a heavy burden
upon Catholics, who must not only build and maintain
school facilities, but must also be ready to expand them as
the Catholic population expands. It should be remembered
as well that more than half the Catholic children of America are not in parochial schools but attend the regular public
school classes and receive their religious education outside
of school in released time or Sunday school programs.

This is the background of the problem of federal aid,
which has become so significant and of such pressing importance during these last years. Most Catholics consider
their position on the subject essentially reasonable. Since
Catholics pay taxes for the education of all young American citizens, they feel that some portion of this tax money
should assist their own children even when these children
do not attend the public schools. The reasoning is based on
the legal supposition that the American school system includes private and independent schools, and not solely the
public schools, as an essential part of the national educational effort. Since school attendance is compulsory and
one fulfills this law by attending any school of recognized

standards, Catholics feel that they may rightfully expect some government aid to be directed to their children when in religious schools.

The Catholic view is supported by argument on many levels. Some appeal to simple justice. A certain amount of money is set aside for the education of young Americans; there is no law that says this education must be a public school education; consequently, the tax money should follow the student wherever he is educated, so that each person's taxes contribute to the education of his own children. Others argue the case on the ground of religious freedom. They point out that Catholics are permitted under the law to send their children to religious schools and that the Supreme Court has upheld this right. They feel that the right is under assault when its exercise means a penalty on those who claim it, as happens when increased taxes for the benefit of public schools take from the family income the means of supporting religious schools. A more recent basis of argument is the public welfare. Government aid to education is currently promoted on the premise of doing the best we can with out national assets, taking advantage of the talents of our young people and making an investment in the future of the United States. Certainly this is a program for all Americans, not just for the percentage who attend public schools. If federal funds are being distributed on this principle, Catholics argue, they should by some formula be apportioned to assist all American youth to develop their abilities for the future benefit of the country.

Behind these and other arguments lies the constitutional question of whether federal assistance may be given to assist institutions operated under sectarian auspices. The Supreme Court has never heard a case on direct federal aid to a private or religious school, and our judgments must therefore be made in connection with peripheral issues which do not strike at the heart of the question. In the McCollum case, for example, the use of school properties for religious education was described as unconstitutional. In the Everson case, bus rides for children attending religious schools were declared constitutional and considered to be an auxiliary service like police and fire protection. The Zorach decision a little later also found constitutional the program of dismissed time where religious education was provided off the school premises. In addition, the Louisiana textbook decision made it legal for the state to provide school books of a nonreligious nature for all the children of the state no matter what schools they attended.

Constitutional lawyers are seldom unanimous on difficult questions, and on federal aid their opinions are divided. Many hold that aid to sectarian institutions even in those areas where religious teaching is not involved is unconstitutional and involves some sort of "establishment." Others, especially in the more recent years, maintain that the law can provide many aids to institutions under religious auspices as well as the people in them without being challenged by constitutional questions. The lines are drawn roughly in this fashion: on the one side are those who feel that justice, religious liberty, public welfare, and rights under the Constitution suggest that federal aid to education should be distributed as widely as possible and not be limited to the nation's public schools; on the other side are those who feel just as strongly that none of these claims is valid and that the Constitution itself makes any kind of federal aid to private or parochial schools impossible.

For many years the Catholic Church had officially opposed all federal aid to education as both dangerous and unnecessary. In their statements over the years the Bishops emphasized that large allotments of federal monies are likely to be followed by an equally large measure of federal control. Like most other Americans, they have been anxious to continue the tradition that allows each state, and in some cases each township, to accept the responsibility for education within its area. They look with suspicion and even alarm at any development suggesting that a national educational policy might be set for every part of the country, with federal control replacing the present generally satisfactory local autonomies.

It is probably fair to say that at the present time most American bishops of the Catholic Church look with disfavor upon the pouring of federal monies into the educational programs of the states. Some people find it difficult to reconcile this general opposition to federal aid with the recent statements of some Catholic leaders urging a Catholic participation in the distribution of educational funds. The explanation is that even though basically they prefer not to have the federal government enter the field of education, Catholics feel that if it should do so, the program should be carried out equitably for the benefit of *all* American schools.

The issue came to its climax in 1961 when President Kennedy presented to the Congress a large educational program which provided monies for colleges and universities of every description but limited those federal monies going to secondary and primary school education to schools conducted under public auspices. Catholics protested what they considered to be discrimination. At a meeting in Washington in November 1961, the Catholic Bishops prepared a statement on this matter which was released by Archbishop Alter:

"Yesterday the Administrative Board met and considered, in addition to routine questions, the particular problems of the Federal Aid to Education. In the absence of the Official Minutes, I think I can summarize the discussions fairly and briefly as follows:

"1. The question of whether or not there ought to be Federal Aid is a judgment to be based on objective economic facts connected with the schools of the country, and consequently Catholics are free to take a position in accordance with the facts.

"2. In the event that there is Federal Aid to Education,

we are deeply concerned that with justice Catholic school children should be given the right to participate.

"3. Respecting the form of participation, we hold it to be strictly within the framework of the Constitution that long-term, low-interest loans to private institutions could be part of the Federal Aid Program. It is proposed, therefore, that an effort be made to have an amendment to this effect attached to the bill.

"4. In the event that a Federal Aid Program is enacted which excludes children in private schools, these children will be the victims of discriminatory legislation. There will be no alternative but to oppose such discrimination."

For the remainder of this session of the Congress the membership was divided on how to find an equitable formula which would satisfy both those who were objecting to aid for religious schools on constitutional grounds and those who were making what they interpreted to be a claim in justice to such aid. The issue was full of emotion and the Congress felt various pressures. Finally, because of the dispute, the President's education bill was locked up in the House Rules Committee, and it became impossible for the Congress to debate the question and then come to a final vote on it. Those blamed most for "killing" the educational aid bill in 1961 were the Catholics, because they had made their position unmistakably clear from the beginning.

The bill was reintroduced again in 1962 and the first voice raised against it was that of Cardinal Spellman, who reiterated his opposition to this kind of discrimination, which, he said, denied the just rights of a large portion of the population and threatened the religious independent school with extinction.

We need not go into questions of constitutionality, or even that more important one of public purpose. Nor do we need to discuss why aid cannot be given directly to citizen children attending religious schools, so that it in no manner touches the institution itself. These and many related questions have been discussed by highly competent scholars over the last years. That a formula can be worked out which will satisfy the demands of all those with legitimate differences appears to be possible, though we cannot expect it to silence those who have less respectable reasons for their position.

Our concern here is the position (and therefore the image) of the Catholic Church as it appears to the American public during this entire controversy. Have Catholics managed to interpret themselves in an intelligible manner to the public at large? Or have positions been taken with less attention to the facts than to traditional postures which have no present relevance to the matter at issue?

Most Americans harbor the impression that Catholics have decided upon a line of action which, regardless of national interest, will favor the fortunes of their Church. Certainly the Catholic Church is the largest religious institution providing education on the elementary and secondary level in the United States and therefore would receive greater sums than other private educational institutions under a general aid program, as the public appreciates. The financial profit from federal aid to schools is not, however, the central issue. The central issue, as already explained, is whether federal monies will be used to assist *all* education on the secondary and primary level in the United States which performs a public function and follows the requirements of the law, or whether it will be limited only to those schools which exist under public auspices and support.

As Americans approach this question, they nearly all come with certain preconceptions. Catholics come with an injured air. They feel, as they have often expressed it, that they are twice taxed, for they must support the American public school system and at the same time pay separately for the education of their children in religious schools. They come, then, with a kind of grudge, a sense of injustice, a feeling that they have been denied what is rightfully theirs. On the other hand many of their non-Catholic neighbors have a very real anxiety over the exceptional growth of religious schools, especially those under Catholic auspices. They feel, and have often expressed their feeling, that these schools are divisive and that they tend to have an unhappy effect on young Americans in them who are withdrawn from the general community life and separated along sectarian lines. Some believe that the public school is the only educational institution worthy of support and that it is the kind of school that makes the best American. Altogether, very few Americans approach this question with anything like a neutral disposition or a willingness to be convinced of views different from those they already hold.

When the positions of those involved in a controversy are already prejudged it is often easy to fancy dangerous postures where they do not exist. These misconceptions are not misrepresentations or misunderstandings so much as assumptions that people have taken positions to which they are not committed.

In the matter of federal aid to education a review of the facts provides quite a different picture from the one that exists in the mind of the average informed American. It is widely believed, for example, that the statement of the Catholic Bishops which opposed the presidential recommendation for aid said that Catholics would oppose the *legislation* when it came before the Congress. To many it seemed that the Bishops had put themselves in the position of saying that unless Catholics received aid for the children in their schools, they would see to it that there was no aid for anyone. The Bishops never held this position, and they took special pains that the document issued in their name announced their opposition not to "legislation" but to "discrimination."

In his many public appearances, the spokesman for the National Catholic Welfare Conference declined to say what position Church authorities would take on the legislation when it appeared. The matter, at this stage, was being argued on principle, not on action. Unfortunately for all of us, the distinction was not clear in the minds of those who reported the issue in the mass media, and it was a good deal less clear in the minds of those who commented upon it in the press or from the pulpit. We do not know whether the Bishops, singly or as a body, would have registered opposition to legislation which would have denied religious schools any federal money. The fact of the matter is that their position in this regard was unrecorded. Judging from the individual statements of the Bishops, it becomes clear that whatever unanimity existed among the members of the Administrative Board did not include every detail of the question.

Writing shortly after the educational aid excitement had subsided, Cardinal Cushing of Boston made his own position public. In a widely quoted statement, which received favorable editorial comment in the *New York Times,* in the *Washington Post,* and elsewhere, the Cardinal declared that aid to Catholic schools should not, in his judgment, be made a condition for permitting the passage of any general aid to education. The Cardinal said:

"While I am not convinced that the Constitution forbids all subsidies to private education, I feel that as long as the majority of the American people are against such use of taxes, Catholics should try to prove their right to such assistance but neither force such legislation through at the expense of national disunity nor use their political influence in Congress to block other legislation of benefit to education because they do not get their own way."

People reading the papers and listening to the commentaries in these months would have believed that the Catholic position was vastly different. They would have been certain that Catholic lobbying in the Congress and the pressure of Catholic votes in the large urban centers were both at work to intimidate members of Congress; they would have been sure that Catholics had decided that there would be no bill at all unless there was one that assisted their schools. Admittedly, Catholic spokesmen had argued that the two issues — general aid and special aid — should be decided together, but this is not the same thing as saying that if one was not granted they would see to it that the other was lost as well.

Noting the scrupulous manner in which Catholic spokesmen in these matters always kept in mind the distinction between policy and action, one may wonder why it was that the image came through with such a lack of clarity. The only explanation is that many of the mass media had so completely made up their minds on what the Catholic position was going to be that they refused to attend closely to what it actually was. Thus the preconceptions so colored the facts that they gave the impression to most Americans that the Catholic Bishops were opposing all federal aid unless an appropriate share was given to Catholic schools; that they were using the national educational need as a stick with which to beat the Congress into getting benefits for their own school children.

Another source of confusion was the Constitution itself. Many Americans began to believe that there was a Catholic constitutional interpretation on the one side and a non-Catholic one on the other, and that the President of the United States had somehow found himself in the non-Catholic camp, probably because he had taken this position during the campaign and could not now change it. It is widely believed that constitutional lawyers hold unanimously that "across the board" benefits to those attending independent schools are unconstitutional. Exactly what "across the board" benefits means has nowhere been made clear. If this expression describes the mass of auxiliary services schools may require, there is nothing like unanimity among constitutional lawyers concerning it.

Attitudes on the constitutional question show no division along religious lines. The President undoubtedly follows the opinions of those whose advice he respects in this matter, and believes now, as he did before he was elected Chief Executive, that benefits of the kind described in the law cannot constitutionally be given to religious and independent schools on the elementary and secondary level. The most widely quoted exponents of the opposing position, that these benefits are compatible with the Constitution, are not members of the Catholic Church. For the most part they are professors of constitutional law at such institutions as the Harvard Law School and the Law School

of the University of Chicago. Naturally, Catholics are quick
to quote the opinions of these distinguished lawyers who
agree with them and whose interpretations would allow
federal aid, and to use them in opposition to the opinions
of equally distinguished jurists and lawyers who hold the
contrary view. The important point is that the experts are
themselves divided and that this division has no relation
whatever to religion but is due to differing legal interpretations of the same historic document.

The misconception that there is a Catholic interpretation
of the Constitution is widespread, and once more there is no
ready answer to the question, why? Perhaps the explanation is that on many questions familiar to the average
American there has always been a "Catholic" position, or
so he supposes, and this experience makes it easy for him to
believe that there is a particular view of the Constitution
which, because of their religious commitments, Catholics
are bound to adopt. Whatever the reason, the fact is that this
opinion is widespread without having any solid basis in
reality.

Another popular misconception relating to federal aid
concerns the Congress. Many commentators in the mass
media took it for granted that Catholic members of the
Congress would be required to assume the same position
as the Bishops — that they would be obliged as loyal Catholics to see that the episcopal wishes were written into law.
If this called for passing a bill providing federal funds for
independent schools, the representatives would have to

vote in favor of such legislation. If it meant that this was going to be denied by the Congress, they would have to vote against *any* kind of aid to *any* kind of school. Counting votes in advance according to religious background was commonplace.

Most Americans believe that the Catholic members of the Congress had no practical alternative. The fact is that there has been, and continues to be, a wide variety of opinion among the various representatives in the Senate and the House who are Catholic. Some are opposed to all aid, some share the President's view that aid to religious schools is unconstitutional, and others believe that it is possible to assist the independent school with a special variety of federal support. These legislators cannot hide their voting records in the past and most of them have been not at all reluctant to make their present position plain. Instead of being a monolithic and homogeneous group who share a single view on the educational issue, Catholics in the Congress represent a rather wide variety of people, from the Speaker of the House, Mr. John McCormack, who favors aid to independent schools, all the way to Senator Jack Miller of Iowa, who does not believe any kind of federal monies should go to any schools.

Many Americans believe that if the Catholic members of the Congress were not to follow the expressed will of the Bishops on any question, they would be visited with swift and effective reprisals. There is no evidence whatever that any member of the Congress has suffered for his position either by public denunciation or by spiritual sanctions against him in the practice of his religion. The President of the United States not only introduced this legislation in 1961 but reintroduced it in 1962 in spite of the clear and often expressed dissatisfaction of the hierarchy. He has not been subjected to any reprisals for having taken the position which is undoubtedly his conscientious and well-studied view. The only explanation of the popular belief is that it fits the Catholic image as it still lingers. Only a stronger effort by Catholics can manage to dispel it.

One other area must be considered in this analysis. The education bill which failed to come to the floor of the Congress was killed in the House Rules Committee by an eight to seven vote. It is widely believed that the vote that made the difference in this committee was that of Representative Delaney from Brooklyn, who expressed himself in no uncertain terms on the matter of discrimination and, supposedly, decided the fate of the federal aid bill for that year. Thus people can say that it was a Catholic, and one of very decided opinion on this question, who made it impossible for the Congress, even if it had wished, to pass the controversial educational legislation.

The record discloses something very different from the popular view. The committee which passed judgment on how to handle the educational bill has fifteen members. Only three are Catholic. Two of the Catholics on the committee voted to bring out the bill. Who, then, was responsible for the fact that it was killed? The answer is that it was killed by the votes of Democratic and Republican Protestants with one Catholic joining.

The opposition to the federal aid bill, for a variety of reasons, was widespread. It was strongly opposed by those who saw in it another wedge in favor of desegregation and integration in the South. It was also opposed by those who thought it an unnecessary expenditure, like the National Association of Manufacturers and the U. S. Chamber of Commerce. It was also opposed by *some* Catholics, who saw in it a weapon of discrimination against them. But it is not fair to place the full burden for its demise on this last group alone. It was, rather, a coalition of people who opposed the bill for a variety of reasons that finally sealed its fate in committee. The popular view, however, continues to see the matter differently, and Mr. Delaney continues to be mentioned as the one who "killed" the educational bill proposed in 1961.

When one inquires why a contrary-to-fact image of the Catholic Church continues to manifest itself whenever a controversial issue arises in our society, we must look back over much of what we have said to find anything like a complete answer. The old image of the Catholic Church in America as self-seeking, power-ridden, obstructionist, and monolithic does not die easily. It retains its force to best advantage when emotion replaces reason, and prejudgment takes the place of recorded fact.

The old image cannot be expected to disappear merely

because it was shattered in the presidential campaign of 1960. It will linger in the back of the minds of many people, and when an issue of consequence comes before the American public, which recalls old fears and woes, it will not be difficult for most people to see again the old caricature.

This places a very special burden upon Catholics and Catholic leadership in the United States. It is not enough to be scrupulously careful, as nearly all spokesmen were in the federal aid to education crisis. Catholics must patiently explain their position in unmistakable terms with an understanding of the audience they are addressing. As the various issues continue to be discussed, there is evidence that the authentic Catholic position is being presented more clearly, especially by the columnists and commentators. The springs of information must be cleared of all past misunderstandings before we can expect the wider American public to receive the Catholic message without distortion. Certainly, the image of the Church will not improve until American Catholics *on every level* make it their concern to interpret the Catholic position in a friendly, forceful, and truthful manner which can be understood and accepted by their non-Catholic American neighbors.